THE CENTURY OF MUSICAL COMEDY AND REVUE

Harry Stone

authorHOUSE®

AuthorHouse™ UK Ltd.
500 Avebury Boulevard
Central Milton Keynes, MK9 2BE
www.authorhouse.co.uk
Phone: 08001974150

First published by AuthorHouse 3/3/2009

ISBN: 978-1-4343-8865-0 (sc)

Printed in the United States of America
Bloomington, Indiana

This book is printed on acid-free paper.

COVER IMAGE:
Disguised to deceive the shareholders: Leslie Henson, Fred Emney and Richard Hearne as fraudulent
directors of Bandits Ltd. in "Going Greek". 1937

CONTENTS

CHAPTER 1
THE FIRST MUSICAL COMEDIES

Affinity is not a word that comes readily to mind when considering the two theatrical genres, musical comedy and revue. Yet it does not require much thought to realise that in practical terms they have much in common.

For a start, in London both were evolved almost simultaneously towards the end of the nineteenth century. Both had almost a century of life.

Then there is the trend for actors to migrate from revue into musical comedy. This is largely because in revue the cast are noticed more for versatility than personality. Once those with star quality had learnt their technique, they moved on to musical comedy. Then they had an entire evening in which to impose their personality; the suave Jack Buchanan, the "motherable" Bobby Howes the masterful Cicely Courtneidge.

Nelson Keyes, was one of the artistes most consistently associated with intimate revue, yet he was never impressive when he walked on stage. His personality seemed almost a blank and this is widely held as the reason for his brilliance in impersonating people.

Indeed, impersonation was another facet which figured prominently in both musical comedy and revue. The other components were the structure, the plot - or rather the absence of it - and, above all, the comedy.

The plot in musical comedy was usually considered a necessary encumbrance. Once a degree of credibility had been established, the curtain to the first act usually fell on a wildly comical situation. No one expected the story to be original. Indeed it was often discarded to re-emerge only in time for the happy ending. For the most part of the evening the author was kept busy dovetailing scenes written for individual members of the cast and specifically for the comedian; his forlorn love for the heroine; the downtrodden little man seen in comparison with the noble, handsome hero. So without some sort of continuity the musical would have become virtually indistinguishable from revue.

Yet the theme for a revue can be as strong or even stronger than for a musical comedy. For instance, in C.B.Cochran's "As You Were" the theme that ran throughout the evening was woman's infidelity to man. It ranged through history from Caesar down to Napoleon. Indeed, Cochran cited Bernard Shaw's "The Apple Cart" as almost the perfection of his idea of revue. It can be the sure touch of a single person, as when Noël Coward provided all the sketches, lyrics and music. Indeed some impresarios had such confidence in the strength of their individual style they incorporated their name in the titles: "C.B. Cochran's Revue of 1926" , "Charlot's Char-a-banc" and George Black's "Black Magic".

Strangely the difference between musical comedy and musical romance, or what today is simply called "a musical", is much greater than between musical comedy and revue. The musical, which remains as popular as ever, has been the subject of much study. This is partly because the music is often closer to operetta and because the story is more credible and indeed, in modern times, can have a realism that is disconcerting rather than glamorous. The comedian has only a small part, if he has a part at all. He provides nothing more than light relief and even then the hand of the producer is usually heavy upon his shoulder.

It was completely different for the comedian in musical comedy. In some instances the author did not supply the comedian with any dialogue at all. His part in the story and the situations in which he found himself were barely sketched in. But he was expected to supply his own jokes and appropriate dialogue.

The best jokes are often topical and soon become stale. One night Arthur Roberts was taken ill. Now his understudy was a conscientious man. Throughout the six weeks "In Town" had been playing at the Prince of Wales, he had stood in the wings noting down every joke Roberts made. On this particular evening, he included them all. The performance lasted an extra hour and a half.

So the happy go lucky, apparently spontaneous atmosphere created by the musical comedy comedian is far too transient to be captured in music or on paper. That is why the lasting memories of a musical comedy tend to stay not with the composer, nor the leading lady but are associated totally with Teddy Payne, W.H. Berry, Leslie Henson or Bobby Howes.

"In Town" is held to be the first musical comedy. It opened at the Prince of Wales in October, 1892. Clement Scott, critic in the "Daily Telegraph", called it "musichalling" the legitimate stage. It was certainly not burlesque and it was not quite the perfected form of musical comedy. But it was nearer the latter than the former.

Paradoxically, the original idea for musical comedy came from a composer, Osmond Carr. But what made it so revolutionary was his suggestion that the cast should be wearing modern dress. Hitherto it had been customary for any piece with music to be in costume. It was this which, for quite some time, prejudiced the highly successful impresario George Edwardes against the idea. But after seeing one of the earliest revues "The Poet and the Puppets", he changed his mind. He commissioned the author, Charles Brookfield, to write a book on the principles laid down by Carr.

Brookfield produced a script consisting of a whole series of amusing situations dovetailed one into another and each devoted to exploiting the skills of the relevant artistes. Almost as though by natural evolution, the artistes started taking liberties with their lines to further their own purposes. Brookfield took extreme exception and refused to continue even though he was only half finished. Ironically, it was this individualism and spontaneity that was to form the very heart of successful musical comedy.

The next step in the evolution of musical comedy was "A Gaiety Girl". It opened in October 1893 not, as might be expected, at the Gaiety but it followed "In Town" at the Prince of Wales. It had several good songs, including "Tommy Atkins" and another Tommy "Tommy on the chute".

Its run of 413 performances finally convinced Edwardes that he had found the right formula. So when it was transferred to The Gaiety, it became the first of a long line of successful shows most with a girl in the title.

Edwardes' formula found full maturity in his next production "The Shop Girl" which opened at the Gaiety in November 1894.

The plot of "The Shop Girl" was taken almost in its entirety from a newspaper report, only in real life the sum was not so astronomical. As a play, though, the plot can hardly be described as outstandingly original. However, being unaccustomed to any plot at all in burlesque, most of the critics were agreeably surprised in discovering a story of any sort. It was about a big hearted millionaire who owes four billion pounds (in today's money) to a pal of his early mining days. He comes to London to look for his friend's daughter who had been left on an orphanage doorstep. He discovers she was working as an assistant in Hooleys Royal Stores, a mixture of Whiteleys and the Army and Navy. The job of identification was designated for some reason to the hero, a poor but worthy medical student. He had the time of his life, lining up all the shop girls for inspection. Proof of identification was a strawberry mark on her shoulder. She turns out to be his fiancée. So they celebrate their good fortune with a princely donation to the aforementioned orphanage and presumably live happily ever after..

And for the first time Edmund Payne was entrusted with the star part, proving he was an able successor to Roberts. Also in the cast was Robert Nainby, who was in practically every Gaiety show for more than twenty years. He specialised in sinister little foreigners and was sure to be lurking wherever conspiracy was afoot. Although it was usually a small part, he always succeeded in making his ominous presence evident.

Willie Warde arranged the dances. He also appeared on stage although it was usually for little more than walking on parts with a line or two. Mime was his strong point so he always had a scene he could develop into quite a long and hilarious bit of business.

Other regular players who joined the company in "The Shop Girl" included Katie Semyour. She was one of the finest dancers then on the light musical stage. She always had a duet with Teddy Payne

GEORGE EDWARDES

Edwardes, or the Guv'nor, as he was generally known, was Irish and born in 1855. His parents had wanted him to go into the Army. Instead he became business manager for one of his relations, Richard D'Oyly Carte. In 1881 he became business manager of the Savoy Theatre where the Gilbert and Sullivan operas were at their zenith. In 1885 he joined John Hollingshead as partner in The Gaiety Theatre. They collaborated over one or two productions till Hollingshead retired leaving Edwardes in full charge.

With the asset of a long line of successes, Edwardes soon had more stars and budding talent than any of his contemporaries. This was despite giving poor salaries. His methods were particularly unusual as he encouraged internal rivalry. For instance, he often employed two composers and two lyrists working independently yet contributing to a single production. Some of his shows even had two leading ladies. Strangely enough this spirit of rivalry never led to unpleasantness back stage. This was partly due to his diplomacy and partly because he chose people with the temperament for working in a team. As a result his stars were quite ready to give up a good bit of business for the sake of the play.

In calling his new type of entertainment musical comedy, Edwardes was careful that comedy should play a dominant role. He considered a clever comedian essential to the piece. So he raised the standards of comedy from the clowning, usual in burlesque, to become a credible character in the piece. He also insisted that, with their new found prominence, his comedians should not be in the customary pantomime kit but be well groomed, well spoken and well dressed. Also he had to be adept. For one thing his comedians usually played a more significant part than in other forms of entertainment. For another it was not enough for the comedian in musical comedy to be just funny; he must also sing and often dance as well. Should he not be endowed with a good singing voice, he would "talk" the verses. It is not a simple technique and was perfected much later by Rex Harrison in "My Fair Lady".

Even so Edwardes was cautious over increasing the emphasis on comedy at the expense of beauty. This was made apparent through the billing. In 1903 while pride of place at the top of the bill went to Gertie Millar, Payne had the next most prestigious place at the bottom, just before the chorus. By 1905 he was listed half way down but had been accorded the much desired single line prefix "and". This gave all the emphasis of a near blank space immediately above. But the even more desired "and" space occurred at the bottom and was still being accorded to the leading lady.

It was through the asset of two brilliant comedians that Edwardes was able in "The Shop Girl" to capture the right mixture of spontaneous high spirits and happy go lucky atmosphere yet have it highly disciplined.

Although it was his last appearance, Arthur Roberts' technique was to influence comedians in musical comedy for the next twenty years. He was the first quick-fire comedian and talked ad lib. He talked very quietly in a clear, staccato voice and with a charming sort of insolence. He kept his audience laughing almost continuously so that sometimes it would actually overlap.

He shared his part in "The Shop Girl" with his former in "In Town" understudy, Teddy Payne. This pair, one just about to retire and the other just about to start a twenty year career as star at the Gaiety, were now working together in perfect harmony. One evening Roberts whispered to Payne that he had completely forgotten about a song they were supposed to interpolate. He could not even remember what the song was about. He told Payne to go ahead and sing his part . It was called "Not a word". Roberts kept repeating the phrase with different emphasis and timing and with such success the audience demanded more and more until Payne had run through all the encore verses. Roberts whispered "Come on Teddy, m'lud, keep your eye on me and we'll make it up as we go along". They ended up with the line: "They say the British lion..." and both struck mute attitudes. The audience was helpless with laughter.

Payne was born in 1865 and had first appeared on the stage at fifteen. But a further nine years were to pass before he made his appearance in the West End. Unlike Roberts his script was provided by the authors and he was always word perfect for the first rehearsal

Teddy Payne was the one exception to Edwardes' insistence that comedians should not be comically dresses. Though he wore grotesque clothes, they were always immaculately tailored in Saville Row. He made up in the same way, no matter what his part, with a tousled red wig with a straight cut fringe in front. He was a neat dancer and sang passably well. He had a lisp but above all he had a comical little face that always seemed surprised and a large mouth which he would purse into every conceivable shape. But basically he relied on his character, the chief component being meekness. He always seemed either to be appreciating all the gifts God had suddenly decided to shower upon him or else bewildered at the misfortune fate seemed equally determined to heap upon him. But above all there was indomitable optimism in the face of overwhelming odds. Like most great comedians, he managed to suggest a sense of pathos beneath all the fun. Typical of the sort of song he would sing was:

The hat that set the fashion for 1892.
Arthur Roberts as Captain Codington in "In Town"

It was an evil hour when I met my Mary Ann,
She was living with her mother on the vegetable plan.
She said if I would try it,
The cold potato diet
I'd regulate my liver and become another man.
Though seriously doubting
I took to brussel sprouting
And now you see what's left of me, a vegetarian.

Following his policy of casting people in pairs, Edwardes made the diminutive Teddy Payne the ideal counterweight to Connie Ediss. She was, to put it lightly, ample and she had no qualms over playing up her bulk. Homely in a sort of way, Connie Ediss had an intrusive and strident jollity. She excelled at point songs, which were rather vulgar, though never offensive and had a trick of suddenly singing tremolo to give a mock pathetic effect. She had studied neither singing nor acting but seemed to have a natural sense of timing which carried her through. Typical of her songs in "The Circus Girl" was.

I think that it's behaving very shabby
For any man to say unpleasant things,
Because I've had some trouble with a cabby
Who went and said I broke his blessed springs.
I haven't ate enough to keep a baby
You do get hungry at a fancy ball,
And there's my husband dashes off a-drinking brandy smashes,
Well, it's not the way to treat a wife at all.

The accent on comedy was further emphasised since the hero was usually termed "a light comedian". He was made credible because he was played as a slightly exaggerated Dude or Johnny. He was a man about town, a type almost literally killed off by the Great War. At the Gaiety he was played initially by Seymour Hicks, then W. Louis Bradfield and, latterly, by George Grossmith. His personality is best summed up in a song:

I'm what folks call a "Johnnie", of the title I am proud.
My manner's always dainty, though my dress a trifle loud.
But I do not shine in anything excepting in the boots,
I've joined the "Junior Pothouse", and drop in when I'm by.
I don't possess much brain, but I have the latest tie.
When I've done my morning Bond Street crawl, I do the thing is style,
And give the cabby half a crown to drive me half a mile.

I'm a patron of the theatre, so jolly, don't cher know
To throw your head back in the stalls and revel in the show.
Shakespeare says "the play's the thing", of course that's awful rot,
I hate a bally tragedy, I loathe a bally plot.
I like to stroll in half way through with no one to object
To sit out half an hour or so don't tax the intellect.
I must confess in "Hamlet" no interest I've found

I much prefer "A Gaiety Girl" or else "Morocco Bound".

For my little pranks at Eton, I have often got the birch.
They ploughed me for the Army and they ploughed me for the Church.
But I've got a little place up North with a tidy roll of rent
So to end my matters properly to Parliament I went.
I represent a borough, I've quite forgot its name,
I never catch the Speaker's eye or ask a question tame.
I never make a rotten speech or even Order call
I find it more effective if you never speak at all.

Far from taking offence, all the dudes in the audience set Grossmith as their ideal. He led the young mens fashions with the cut of his coat, the lapel line or the slope of the pockets. This was largely because the characters he played on stage were surrounded by pretty girls and they would have dearly loved to be in his place. But above all, both Hicks and Grossmith had character and personality the audience could believe in. They had all the poise of a man about town and their very lack of acting technique led the dudes to believe they themselves could cut just as an attractive personality. Grossmith in particular, could not lay any claims to good looks..

The Dude and the Dupe. George Grossmith and Teddy Payne
in "The Girls of Gothenburg" in 1907

He was not a good dancer, being rather stiff limbed and apt to use his elbows and he was certainly not a good singer. But he knew how to put a song over with all the necessary zest. What he lacked in nuance he made up in speed and attack. His jokes were topical and spiced with wit. Yet he never went out of his way to emphasise a point to get a laugh. Indeed he never seemed to expect people to laugh at all but let the humour follow naturally. A typical Dude remark was made by G.P.Huntley to a waitress "I say, you do pour tea well, right into the cup every time". It was only because of all these modest attributes, his good temper and the assumption he could keep the heroine far above the manner to which she was accustomed, that the audience was prepared to accept her marrying such an unmitigated nincompoop

Indeed Edwardes encouraged all the principals to make spontaneous and topical jokes. As a result they would scour the evening papers for suitable subjects and then send the call boy with the message that Mr. so and so sends his respects and begs to reserve such and such. On this the recipient would try and guess what the joke was going to be and work out something to cap it.

Nor did the company necessarily refrain from playing jokes on one another actually on stage. George Graves has told how one evening he missed his cue. When, eventually, he did put in an appearance, Robert Evett greeted him with the disconcerting remark "Ah, you're late, we've been waiting for you". However nothing daunted, Graves launched into his usual string of anecdotes. But the audience did not so much as titter. Evett watched his growing discomfort with evident amusement. Eventually he interrupted with "Yes, yes, we told them all that while we were waiting for you". The audience, suddenly grasping the situation, gave the loudest laugh of the evening.

Then not only the official lyrist but also the more talented members of the cast, were themselves writing topical encore verses. With songs such as "Peace, Peace" from "A Country Girl", the world was the limit:

There's a lady today, in the great USA
Who declares she is ready to take on
Any critics who try to dispute or deny
That our Shakespeare is written by Bacon.
For if only you look at the page of a book
Where the errors of printing are rifer
You will find that they tell some improbable tale
In the Bacon Bilateral Cipher.

There's a writer of rhymes that appear in "The Times"
Who is down upon football and cricket.
He pours out his soul on the oaf at the goal
Or the flannelette fool at the wicket.
There was violence afeared when his verses appeared
But the poet was no idle dreamer
When the oafs in the mud came to look for his blood
He was off to the Cape in a steamer.

Edwardes always had the initial germ of an idea for a piece which he would pass on to his authors. Even after they had completed the script, Edwardes would make drastic changes. In one instance, the authors had arranged for the wife of a philanthropist to catch him secretly dining with a music hall artiste. Admittedly the situation was not particularly novel, but at least it was effective - that is until Edwardes decided to turn the wife into four daughters. Similarly during the course of rehearsals, Edwardes would find fault with almost every line in the piece and have it re-written. So really it was surprising the plots were not ironed out completely.

The long suffering resident author was James Tanner. He had led an amazing life. Born in 1859 he had at one time been so utterly poor he had been forced to sleep out on the Embankment. He had graduated to authorship via scene painting, stage management and acting. This varied experience had taught him all the subtleties of play construction. Tanner once flattered himself by claiming "My plots are made up of funny situations". He would, perhaps, have been nearer the mark had he said his plots had situations in which the comedians could be funny.

One of the fundamental problems with musicals, comedy or romance, is to arrange for characters in a modern setting to burst into song. Edwardes felt it acceptable if most of the lyrics were describing character or situation.

It was a fundamental approach which was still being practised in the sophisticated musicals of Rodgers and Hammerstein in the 'fifties such as "I'm Just a Girl who Can't say No" in "Oklahoma!" and "This was a Jolly Fine Clam-Bake" in "Carousel"

Most of these lyrics were written by Adrian Ross, one of the best lyrists of this time. His real name was Arthur Reed Ropes. He was a very mild looking Cambridge don, Fellow of Kings College, a lecturer on history and a veritable encyclopaedia of general knowledge. He had written a volume of serious verse and Edwardes considered his work as good as the Ingoldsby Legends. He took the writing of rhymes no less seriously. He preferred to have his words set to music and if required, he could produce all sorts of tricks and metrical subtleties and even, if required, Quadra syllabic rhymes. But he was always mindful that lyrics in musical comedies can be too clever and he firmly remained popularly witty. He would normally write words to the music when the composer had a good tune. For the comic songs and duets he would prefer to write the words first. For the sentimental songs it was "whichever came first".

Edwardes was against having music in the style of the tiresome ballades usual in historical romances. He demanded it should be set more in the catchy style of the music hall; lively and tuneful, almost inviting the audience to join in. Only the grand finales at the end of each act approached light opera.

Edwardes himself had no ear for music and could not even hum in tune. Yet he knew exactly what he wanted and could tell if a song was likely to be a success. Perhaps this was why he could be just as ruthless with the score and had no compunction over cutting a song or interpolating a new one.

His resident composer at the Gaiety was Lionel Monckton. He had been music critic for "The Daily Telegraph" and proved he could be just as hard in criticising his own work. He would set and re-set a lyric over and over again. He knew his limitations and would never tackle anything that was beyond him. Robert Courtneidge has described his habit of "coming into a rehearsal in an aloof fashion, scarcely greeting anyone and, apparently as he watched the proceedings, taking but little interest in its progress. Between times he would sit down at the piano and run over some of the music he had composed, whilst the words or business of the play were being rehearsed. Every now and then I would beg him to be quiet, but still the playing would continue in a more subdued fashion. Suddenly we, who rehearsed, would become aware that something new and tuneful was emerging from the familiar melodies. The work would be stopped and inquiries made as to what it was. The answer was invariably evasive and, slowly hoisting himself up from the piano with a look blended of boredom and indifference, quietly whistling to himself, would wander out of the stage door without further word to anyone. This was a little comedy he loved to play.

"When rehearsals were well advanced and a number either to replace an unsatisfactory one or in a situation not provided for, was urgently needed, out would come that which we had heard. His critical eye had foreseen the necessity and provided for it so that his best efforts came in at the finish."

This extraordinary emphasis on improvisation and extemporization would have been disastrous had not Edwardes been able to impart a particular style. It gave all the isolated, inconsequential scenes a unity. For instance, everything, right down to the smallest prop, had to be of the finest quality. As a result, his productions were always in impeccable taste. He worked at high speed. He had an eagle eye for dullness and was careful never to let a rehearsal develop into a grind. As soon as a particular scene looked like becoming stale he would give it a rest for a day or two.

This state of continuous flux lasted not only through rehearsals but during the actual run. There were no preliminary tours so the pieces were usually quite undistinguished when they first opened. They gained the distinctive quality only after the first few weeks. Each night Edwardes would watch the audience's reaction and cut out anything when their interest flagged. And as the piece would be pulled together, some parts would be elaborated others whittled down and some completely eliminated.

Even after he felt he had got it right he would still continue altering and improving.

The result was a strange mixture of cleverness and carelessness which was absolutely in keeping with his lackadaisical preparation. So taking all in all, after a production had been running for about a year not only the story but also the score would be altered beyond all recognition. Due to this constant change in both production and comedy, the more ardent fans would see a show literally dozens of times.

These daily changes could be easily made for Edwardes had a healthy respect for the power of the Lord Chamberlain. Also he knew the audience would vigorously protest if he included anything lewd. And this was still in the years before George Bernard Shaw shocked audiences with the word "bloody". Even when Edwardes transgressed the social line and mentioned the Prince of Wales, no matter how innocently, H.R.H. made his displeasure known in no uncertain way.

"The Shop Girl" ran for 546 performances. This was a big success for those days. Even so there were still those who said that musical comedy was just a passing phase.

"My Girl" followed in July 1896 and ran for a disappointing 183 performances. Nearly everything about it seemed to be not quite so good as "The Shop Girl". It had poor music, though this time it was by Osmond Carr, not Monckton. Tanner provided rather careless dialogue for a muddled plot involving Jewish financiers, simple minded parsons, naive daughters, gold mines and the stock exchange.

"My Girl" was followed in December by "The Circus Girl". It was based on a German play which was, in turn, based on a farce. Several people had a hand in writing the musical version, but the guiding one was James Tanner. Despite all this pedigree, the plot of "The Circus Girl" was very trite. In fact, by far the most amusing part was the sub plot. Somehow it came about that Teddy Payne had to challenge the champion wrestler, known as "The Terrible Turk", in order to win enough money to marry Katie Seymour. First he timidly tried to make friends with the Turk. But that was no good. So in desperation he managed to get the Terrible Turk terribly drunk. When the contest began, Teddy Payne barely had to touch him before he fell down for the count whilst the curtain was slowly lowered. But it quickly rose again to show the Turk, now fully conscious, hotly pursuing Teddy Payne into the wings.

The next piece was "The Runaway Girl", which was produced in May 1898. Lionel Monckton contributed a song that became a classic "Soldiers in The Park" more usually known by its first line "Oh, Listen to the Band". "The Runaway Girl" was replaced by "The Messenger Boy" in February 1900. Again the idea for the piece came from real life. A messenger boy called Jaggers (Tom Bang in the Gaiety version played by Teddy Payne) made a dramatic voyage across the Atlantic to fulfil his errand. Such a subject gave boundless opportunities and by the end of the evening, the Gaiety Tom Bang had visited Brindisi, Cairo and Paris. During the course of his travels, Teddy Payne did some astonishing spoof conjuring tricks before Hooka Sasha and his court only too well aware that if he made a slip, he would be subjected to horrible punishment. He finished his performance with a furious dervish dance. Then, together with Katie Seymour, he mimed the average day in the life of a policeman, a sailor, a soldier and a fireman. It was the last time Teddy Payne and Katie Seymour were to sing a duet before she retired from the stage. It was one of the best pieces they ever did together. They also appeared as Ramses and Queen Hatasu, complete with wooden sunshades to sing "Mummies". Another song "Maisie" was sung by Rosie Boote. It was strangely prophetic for one of the lines ran "someday I mean to wed a duke - don't doubt me" and she was not far wrong for it was during the run of "The Messenger Boy" that she married the Marquess of Headfort. It was the first of a whole spate of marriages between the chorus and the peerage.

The next piece was "The Toreador", again by James Tanner, which opened in June 1901. Queenie Leighton was a flashing Spanish beauty, wanted by the police. But, as the critic in the "Sketch" remarked, "no wonder since the police are human". "The East End and the West" was a prime example of the duets between Teddy Payne and George Grossmith who had just taken over the juvenile lead.

"The Toreador" ran for 675 performances making it the most successful run the Gaiety ever had.

Things were changing, though, and the old theatre was destined to be pulled down in deference to a planning scheme. So towards the end of the run, the second act was replaced by "The Linkman" which was, in effect, a revue of the past Gaiety shows

The new Gaiety theatre opened in October, 1903 under the best augurs for their Majesties King Edward VII, Queen Alexandra and Princess Victoria attended the first night. The piece was called "The Orchid"

It was really a glorified old Gaiety burlesque. Teddy Payne was, as usual, the star and confirmed the precedent begun in "The Toreador" of a duet with George Grossmith. This time it was about the unemployed.

It was in this piece that Gertie Millar had her first really important part. She was one of the most famous leading ladies in all musical comedy. Her personality seemed simply boundless though her abilities were strictly limited. She did not comply to the conventional type of beauty except for her saucy little nose. She had a slim but delicate figure but really her charms were not physical. Her attraction lay in her good nature and the spirit with which she entered into anything happening on stage. At the same time she had charming simplicity which endeared her to the audience, who took her straightway to its heart. She half sang, half spoke the songs in a sweet but tiny breathless voice, so that it was often difficult to catch the words. Normally she would never have been heard. But directly she came on stage, a complete hush would fall on the house. But for all this apparent naivety, she could invariably judge how to put over a part or a song to the best effect. Her seemingly effortless movements made her dancing look almost ethereal.

Grossmith now succeeded James Tanner as author of the books of the Gaiety shows. Like Tanner he was quite agreeable for his work to be altered, even if it was at the request of an artiste. He abandoned the melodramatic influence and concentrated more on the farce. In order to give the piece at least a semblance of probability, he would construct it around some recent sensational event. In this he owed more than a nodding acquaintance with intimate revue.

"The Spring Chicken" opened in May 1905. People were extremely entente cordiale conscious just then, so Grossmith chose to adapt a French piece and, indeed, a French cause celebre. It was about a lawyer, Babari, an obvious travesty of Labori, one of the lawyers who had defended Dreyfus. As Labori, Grossmith was, for most of the year, a respectable man and the model of all propriety. But when Spring was in the air, discretion was thrown to the winds.

However Edwardes had begun to feel the Gaiety formula was growing thin and needed a change. So just for the next piece he recalled Tanner, who complied with "The New Aladdin", which opened in September 1906. It bore the official description of an "extravaganza". Although "The New Aladdin" ran for 203 performances it seemed to owe too much to burlesque to be really popular.

With "The Girls of Gothenburg" in May 1907, Grossmith was recalled as author. He based the piece on the recent exploits of a German cobbler Koepenick. He had taken advantage of the German foible for holding the military in the highest esteem by masquerading in an officer's uniform. In the Gaiety version, the Blue Hussars were stationed at Rottenburg. Rottenburg was indeed rotten. There was only one girl in all the town - even though she was Kitty Mason, so the Hussars found life very dull. So did the audience who were disappointed that the girls did not appear until the second scene. However, Teddy Payne as Max Moddelkopf put all that right when he arrived with a dispatch from the Kaiser - spoofed of course. It ordered the regiment to Gothenburg. Gothenburg turns out to be the opposite of Rottenberg for there is a college full of young ladies. Connie Ediss had left. But in compensation the chorus now included Gladys Cooper.

After "The Girls of Gothenburg" had finished its London run it was taken over, almost complete, to New York, but it did not meet with much success.

Fortunately, with the production of "Our Miss Gibbs" in January 1909, everything was back to normal. The old company where home again with Gertie Millar, George Grossmith and Teddy Payne.

Although the authorship of "Our Miss Gibbs" was attributed to Cryptos, George Grossmith undoubtedly had more than a little say in its construction. It was right up to date again, being centred around the stealing of the Ascot Gold Cup, an incident that had happened the previous season. Teddy Payne was Gertie Millar's cousin up from Yorkshire. He had come up to London to take part in a brass band competition.

The second act was set at the White City during the World Athletic Championships. All are ready waiting for the finish of the marathon. Excitement is at fever pitch when on staggers a little figure in white running shorts. He is acclaimed winner and enthusiastically chaired by the cheering crowd. Then it is found there has been a mistake and it is only Teddy Payne. The mob sought revenge by ducking him.

Then followed a scene of bewitching enchantment, the sort of scene which lives in the memory for a lifetime. In the dim light, eight pierrots, dressed in light blue, are a-tumble on the stage. On bounds a small, lithe figure with a huge white bow tied beneath the chin. Then in a familiar and so loved voice, the ditty is more felt than heard through the half light: "I'm such a silly when the moon comes out". "Moonstruck" was one of Monckton's best remembered tunes and Gertie Miller's best remembered songs..

For once Grossmith refused to make any alterations after the first night and "Our Miss Gibbs" was one of the best shows Edwardes ever staged. It ran for 636 performances.

But it turned out to be the crest before the trough. The company was breaking up. Gertie Millar left for "The Quaker Girl". Lionel Monckton moved with her to the Adelphi and Adrian Ross also left.

When the First World War was declared Edwardes was in Germany and was repatriated through the intervention of the American Consul. Nevertheless he was a broken man and died shortly after his return.

GEORGE DANCE

The only other person who could lay claim to having invented musical comedy was George Dance. His lack of recognition is largely because his main interest lay in touring the provinces. But though the few musicals he did produce in London are interesting, they did not enjoy anything like the same popularity. They were not in the least influenced by Edwardes's productions. For instance, he did not attach such importance to the chorus. However, they shared the opinion that a comedian is vital.

Dance himself was responsible for a large part of all his shows. He not only produced them but wrote the books and also the lyrics which were definitely of the music hall genre.

I know a certain boarding house
Not far from Russell Square
The neighbourhood is charming
With extremely bracing air.
The terms are one one one weekly
That's inclusive board and bed
But a guinea's not expensive
To be warmed and housed and fed.
But when the dinner's cleared away
I'm told the boarders roar
For a tough old hen won't nourish ten
And I hear they want some more.
They've ping-pong in the drawing room
But precious little more
And boarders come and boarders go
Though n'ere returning more
But from "The Daily Mail" today
I hear they want some more.

Many of Dance's musical comedies were based on fairy tales adapted for adults. He always wrote them to exploit the personality of the comedian.

It is "A Modern Don Quixote" which holds a rival claim with "In Town" to be the pioneer musical comedy. It was produced by Dance a year later at the old Strand Theatre in September 1893. It was officially described on the programme as a "nondescript". But it was only a month later that Edwardes produced a similar sort of entertainment in the form of "A Gaiety Girl" and christened it musical comedy

"A Modern Don Quixote" depended almost entirely on Arthur Roberts, who had been such a success in "In Town". Amongst other things in the show he mimed not only a young swell at supper but the dependable old waiter serving him. Later he went on to show a young lady setting her hair with such realism one could actually guess the style of coiffure.

Dance next produced "The Lady Slavey" at the Avenue, in October 1894. It was an adaptation of the Cinderella story. The mainstay was the comedienne May Yohe. She had a strange contralto voice but only a range of five or six notes. So Dance wrote all her songs especially for her.

In April 1896 Dance presented "The Gay Parisienne" at the Duke of Yorks. It saw the debut of one of Dance's greatest protégés Lois Freer . The whole production depended on her. She was a tiny woman, practically a dwarf, with a funny little face and a funny sort of walk. In "The Gay Parisienne" she sang "Sister Jane's Top Note". On one occasion she acted an entire scene with her back to the audience. The audience was in complete hysterics. Yet no one was quite sure whether she did it on purpose or whether she had become so excited she did not realise.

In October 1901, George Dance produced "A Chinese Honeymoon" at the old Strand Theatre. It was the first time a West End production ran for over a thousand performances, 1,075 to be precise. Having toured the provinces for some months, the London production opened with a polish unusual in the West End. The long run was in part because it succeeded in drawing audiences from the East End as well as the West End.

Dance had no compunction in completely ignoring all Chinese conventions and precious few people cared anyway. He took pains to provide convincing characters and a competent plot with a love story that was not too intrusive. Even if a lot of the situations were rather silly, they were excusable because they were made amusing

A Mr. and Mrs. Pineapple go to China for their honeymoon. Much to Mr. Pineapple's dismay, his wife insists on bringing all four of her bridesmaids . While that could have been acceptable, for they were all very pretty, she also provided them with whistles to blow whenever Mr. Pineapple seemed in danger of straying from the path of strict fidelity.

As a sub plot, there was the Emperor of China, determined to find a bride. His subjects, fearful of their lives, hurriedly submit Lois Freear, she being under a misapprehension over the whole business. There could have hardly been a more ill assorted couple, with Picton Roxborough, the tallest actor then on the London stage as the Emperor and the diminutive Lois Freear as his slave fiancée. Lois Freear had three songs which were in Dance's best manner: "Matha Spanks the Grand Piana", "The twiddly Bits" and "I want to Be A Lady".

Certainly George Dance has a fair claim to having invented musicals and having also met with a certain measure of success. But taking an overall view, there can be no doubt that George Edwardes had the more lasting influence on musical comedy.

CHAPTER II
SPECTACULAR REVUE

The one major factor musical comedy and spectacular revue have in common is a large chorus of pretty girls.

It was John Hollingshead, manager of the old Gaiety who discovered that an admirer of a pretty girl would patronise a stall night after night. He was foolish enough to admit openly that he set more store to a chorus girl's legs than her voice - and he was expelled from his Club for saying so. But he was undoubtedly right. He was, though, prepared to compromise to a degree and would have one or two competent singers tucked away in the back row.

Hollingshead also initiated what came to be known as "the big eight". They were tall and statuesque girls who gave stance to the proceedings during the light scenes with comedians and the undiluted sentiment of the juveniles. But they never acted. In fact they never did anything more than enhance the scenery and smile at the audience.

George Edwardes continued this policy but he groomed them to be more lady like. He made them sing a little and dance a few easy steps. He also made them learn French and fencing for poise. He emphasised what W. Macqueen Pope aptly called "that aura of feminine allure "by dressing them in long skirts and frou-frous instead of the tights and near nudity of burlesque. As a result, instead of attracting over aged oglers in the front rows, the sprigs of society started favouring a particular girl. They would come each night and leave expensive bouquets which often contained invitations to supper. So when the performance was over, the "Johnnies" would have their broughams waiting outside the stage door and whisk their charmer to supper at Romanos (unsafe), Rules (also unsafe) or The Savoy (safe). So it was hardly surprising several of the girls married into the peerage. Besides Rosie Boote there were Sylvia Storey who became the Countess of Poulett and Olive May who became the Countess of Drogheda. It was Ruby Miller's health that was drunk in champagne out of her slipper by an Eastern Potentate. When she complained that her shoe was damp he next day sent her two dozen pairs in every sort and shade of material.

The third major exponent of the chorus girl, after Hollingshead and Edwardes, was Paul Derval who took over the Folies Bergere in Paris. Completely independently he had come to appreciate how beautiful girls could enhance his gorgeous sets as well as attract the patrons.

As it happened, George Grossmith was invited to Paris by Derval. The experience made its mark and in due course he was to adopt much of the Parisienne formula in his series of spectacular revues at the Empire Theatre

At about this time, Florence Ziegfeld, a small time producer in New York, had also realised the potential of the formula. After a tentative experiment, he went big time with a series of

Follies. And then there was Albert de Courville. He had travelled all over Europe and America and had seen both The Folies Bergere and the New York Follies. He incorporated the best from both worlds in a series of revues at the London Hippodrome.

GEORGE GROSSMITH

George Grossmith came from a fortunate family. George senior had more or less drifted from amateur dramatics into professional appearances at Institute dinners. There he had been discovered by W.S.Gilbert and recruited for the Savoy Opera Company. George Junior was studying for the Army when Gilbert offered him a part in a new play. The salary was 2.5 pounds but George senior said it was too much for such an inexperienced actor and had it cut to one pound.

On the opening night of "Morocco Bound", George Grossmith had a part of three lines. After 300 performances, his part had become the largest in the piece. He accomplished this by gagging, ad libbing and on the slightest provocation breaking into elaborate mime. At first the cast had merely given him hostile stares. But when this had no effect on this impertinent young pup, they put him in his place by making disconcerting jokes at his expense. But Grossmith proved immune to their barbs. Every time they scored a point he would retreat into a high pitched giggle and this invariably topped the laugh. The part of Lord Percy Pimpleton in "Morocco Bound" was to type cast Grossmith Junior as the Dude of the Gaiety musicals.

When in 1905 Grossmith took charge of the Empire Theatre, the bill consisted mainly of variety turns with one or two episodes given over to the newly invented bioscope. So Grossmith introduced revue to form a third and dominant part of the programme. However largely due to the jealousy of some of his contemporaries, the London County Council introduced several ridiculous restrictions. The revue must not last longer than 20 minutes. It must not have more than six characters. Grossmith did eventually manage to have this last increased to twelve.

The first Grossmith revue at The Empire was "Rogues and Vagabonds". Even with the larger cast he still had to have each person playing four or five parts. One of the most popular sketches was Kitty Hanson, Elsie Clare and Harry Grattan as three chorus girls, but appearing in different disguises, usually politicians, every night. Grossmith also incorporated the true to life spectacular set much used in melodrama. In this case it was the Aldwych which had just emerged as part of the Kingsway development.

In "Venus 1906", Grossmith had the goddess overhear a peer lauding the susceptibilities of the Gibson Girl. This creation from the imagination of an American cartoonist with her impossible "hour glass" figure had become the rage of the town. With Vulcan as her witness, Venus brings an action for insulting behaviour. This gave good cause for a fine interior scene of the Law Courts. It also conveniently lent itself to a procession of impersonations taking the witness stand. The scenic piece de resistance, however, was Trafalgar Square. Not content with showing it covered in snow, Grossmith had Vulcan loose her temper, stamp her elegant foot, whereupon then and there and in full view of the audience, the whole square began to disintegrate.

Next at the Empire Theatre, George Grossmith proffered "Oh Indeed" which opened in 1908. Valli Valli parodied an undressing scene in the sensation play of the season, "Diana of the Dobson's".

Other revues Grossmith wrote for the Empire included "Come Inside" in 1909 and "Hullo London" the year after. Maud Jay satirised Lady Constance Stewart-Richardson who was always dancing for charity She was snubbed "Why not dance where charity begins?" Cuthbert Clarke wrote the music, which included "Shine on Harvest Moon". He went on to provide the score for three more Empire revues including "By George", being Grossmith of course, and in 1912 "Everybody's Doin' it".

In this case Grossmith delegated most of the acting to Robert Hale. He appeared as Lord Lonsdale and the Surrey and England cricketer P.G.H.Fender, complete with goggles, long nose and outsize sweater. But he provoked the loudest response when he appeared as a Master of Foxhounds. He rode a spirited hobby horse and was accompanied by a pack of stuffed hounds. It never failed to evoke hunting cries from the audience

After this Grossmith transferred his allegiance to the Alhambra, opening in October 1912 with "Kill That Fly". This was his first revue to make up an entire programme. He took Robert Hale with him who again provided an equestrian streak in "Ascot Ups and Downs". It showed the racecourse furnished with numerous Heath Robinson contraptions including mechanical boots to urge the horses to a quick start. Grossmith was also first in satirising the new influx of American musicals. It was the start of what rapidly became an essential part of every revue.

Now that Grossmith had the Alhambra on an even keel he handed most of the production work over to the young manager Andre Charlot. Charlot was already highly experienced, having worked in several Parisian theatres including the Folies Bergers. Grossmith did, though, retain responsibility for the scripts since the trouble with the LCC persisted. Shortly after, he succeeded in getting the maximum playing time doubled to sixty minutes. Conversely his expertise prompted him to increase the sense of speed by making the sketches shorter. In fact he halved them from an average ten minutes down to five.

Grossmith also abolished the French practice of compère and commère, who were constantly on stage, introducing and commenting on the various sketches. They, too, slowed the production. So in May 1913 in his next revue "Eightpence a Mile" (the standard fare for the London cabby), he had the compère and commère incorporated into the sketches. Set a hundred years ago, Robert Hale, as Lord Haymarket, takes Phyllis Monkman as Miss Gertie Gaiety, a girl up from Lancashire, on a tour round London. They set out in the afore mentioned cab but get no further than Admiralty Arch before they realise there is something peculiar . There are aeroplanes flying about. They are in the future. While that was about as far as any coherent sequence was concerned, it marked the start of Grossmith's successful writing collaboration with Fred Thompson.

The programme described Phyllis Monkman in her part of Miss Gertie Gaiety as an exotic dancer. But over the subsequent productions, she proved to be much more than that. In the exotic parades, that had by now become an inevitable part of every spectacular revue, she was on every cap the very button. In the banquet she appeared as caviar; in the avery she was the peacock and in the garden she was the English Rose.

Robert Hale abandoned Lord Haymarket to become a modern variety artist. He started telling off latecomers but to his considerable discomfiture they start answering back. He then realises some of them are his relations so he invites them to come up on stage. Furthermore one of the programme girls tells him she has discovered kinship with a policeman who also joins

*Phyllis Monkman as the butterfly caught in Carlotta Mossetti's spider's web in
"Eight pence a Mile" in 1913*

them on stage. They formed a motley and highly vociferous ensemble. Hale also impersonated the silent picture comedian Charles Prince in his most famous part Wiffles. There was another law courts scene but this time as a skit in its own right. The barristers, jury and attendants laughed dutifully long and uproariously at every feeble quip made by the judge. "A Musical Dream" was designed with a black and white surround as a foil for the centrepiece made up with all the colours of the prism. Then there were dancers invisible against the black back drop except for their white hats, gloves and walking sticks.

"Keep Smiling" which followed in October 1913 included Lee White. Her immediate appeal was an infectious sense of humour. Though her songs were also usually humorous they were often tinged with pathos. Godfrey Tearle also joined the cast of "Keep Smiling", trailing all the glamour acquired as a matinee idol. Once again Robert Hale raised most of the laughs. He appeared as a lady gifted with second sight though it soon transpired her sight was seriously blurred. There was also a young lady who sang some songs and performed rather undistinguished male impersonations in the style of Hetty King. Her name was Beatrice Lillie. Another entry of incidental interest on the programme was the press officer, C.B.Cochran.

Grossmith took the title of the next production which opened in May 1914 from the sensational line in the latest work by George Bernard Shaw. But though "bloody" had been permitted by the Lord Chamberlain, delicacy restrained Grossmith from incorporating it in "Not Likely". It did, however, include a dance version of "Pygmalion". The highly effective finale had the whole cast making their exit up four walkways zigzagging from stage to flies. Not that Grossmith had much to do with this particular revue at all. With Andre Charlot as his highly competent manager and the book in the hands of E.L.Barman and Cosmo Gordon-Lennox, Grossmith was able to turn his attention to becoming an impresario in his own right. His first two productions, "Peg o My Heart" and "Potash and Perlmutter" were major successes.

So the next Alhambra revue also became largely the responsibility of Andre Charlot. The title was taken from the box office telephone number "Five 0 Six Four Gerrard". The book was again by Cosmo Gordon-Lennox. This time he was assisted by Robert Hale who, of course, also remained the main prop of the company

In keeping with the title, the sketches were presented as a series of telephone calls. In two of them Robert Hale focussed on J.M. Barrie. First he impersonated the leading lady in Barrie's only - and disastrous, - essay into musical comedy "Rosy Rapture, the Pride of the Beauty Chorus". Then he appeared as Gaby Delys receiving the attentions of Jack Morrison as Barrie. He was in a very short kilt, because, he was at pains to explain, he understood brevity to be the soul of wit.

Beatrice Lillie was beginning to develop her comic brilliance. She was a pantomime principle boy, evidently owing her promotion less to ability than the shortage of men due to Army recruitment. Then, staying with the army and reverting to her male impersonations, she sang "What shall we do with them down on the farm now that they've seen gay Paree?"

Phyllis Monkman appeared in a bear dance with a Mr. Magley as the bear. Her high spot in the evening, however was even more erotic, though claiming educational value as a scholarly study of the sun worshiping Incas of Peru.

The Great War brought about a startling change in the type of West End audience. The initial reaction of the London managements had been almost to apologise for providing levity in such times of trouble. Revue, in particular, felt it important to incorporate morale boosting patriotism. There were quantities of patriotic songs sung by inspiring uniformed choruses. There was self conscious disparaging of the enemy. either with incompetent spies or a grotesque Kaiser.

It took a year or two for impresarios to realise that a large proportion of the audiences were made up of servicemen on leave. They did not want this. One night Grossmith noticed two acquaintances with girl friends in one of the boxes. After the show, he upbraided them on such extravagance saying he would have gladly given him four stalls.

"No, this is special. We go back to the front tomorrow. Where we are there isn't a chance in ten thousand." Four days later their names were on the list of those killed in action.

Then there was a woman who frequently bought two seats for matinees of "Chu Chin Chow". The other seat was always empty. A curious management at last asked her why. "My son", she replied, "loved the piece. He was killed on the Somme and I always place his cap on the seat beside me and I feel he is with me enjoying the show"

The men at the front did not really sing "Tipperary" "Pack up your Troubles" and all the other songs tailor made for them by dutiful songwriters. They sang songs from the hit West End musicals: "If You Were the Only Girl in the World" and "They'll Never Believe me".

So the impresarios shaped their productions to provide the escapism demanded. The enormous success of the oriental spectacular "Chu Chin Chow" showed that opulent settings in a country deprived of extravagance were nothing to be ashamed of since it pleased the boys home on leave. The war had also made audiences more cynical. Up to now the sketches had been comparatively unsophisticated. Producers now realised they must be considerably sharpened.

The Alhambra was undergoing a complete change. Andre Charlot moved to the Playhouse where he staged the first of what turned out to be a long line of his own successful revues. With him went Beatrice Lillie, whom he was soon to build up into the great comedienne

Robert Hale returned to the Alhambra to appear in "Follow the Crowd".

George Grossmith joined the RNVR. He described his duties as acting as messenger boy. Certainly they gave him strange licence for he was able at the same time to continue in the theatre.

He began work with Fred Thompson on an adaptation, in its broadest sense, of an idea by the French satirist Rip. With it they brought back the traditional French compère, Violet Loraine as the knowledgeable Emma McKay and two commères, George Robey and Fred Lester as Lucifer and Oliver, the brothers known as "The Bing Boys". The prologue showed them as country bumpkins at Binghampton when news arrives that Emma, the cook who had left for London, has made her name on the stage. At Lucifer's insistence, a reluctant Oliver accompanies him up to Town where Emma is waiting to show them the sights. Included was a visit to the Mappin Terrace at the Zoo. There they saw a dancing golden pheasant called Phyllis Monkman,

Before long Lucifer has fallen blindly in love with Emma. He feels he ought to serenade her, but he has no voice. However he installs brother Oliver behind a screen in her dressing room and mimes the words. What a song and, indeed, what a score for it was by Nat D. Ayer and included "I stopped, I Looked and I Listened", "Another little Drink wouldn't do us any harm" and, of course, "If I was the Only Boy in the World". As though this was not sufficient, Ivor Novello contributed several interpolations including a skit on his enormously successful "Keep The Home Fires Burning".

As Lucifer, George Robey was all roguishness and daring. He had already built up a formidable reputation on the halls. It was this experience that made him one of the few comedians capable of controlling the large Alhambra audiences. He had that rare authority whereby he could command laughter or silence at will. If, occasionally, the laughter grew out of control or he made an even more outrageous double meaning, he would stare at them looking as though completely baffled as to what they were finding so funny.

Alfred Lester proved an excellent foil as Oliver. Physically he was a complete contrast; thin, small and ever so sad. Lester had always specialised in lugubrious parts ever since he had made his name as the doleful jockey in the musical "The Arcadians". It was not so much that unfortunate things happened; he was always expecting that. No, even if everything was going well, he still feared the fickleness of fate was promising disaster.

Between these two there was Violet Loraine as the former cook and new star. She brought the breath of sanity between the extremes of the two brothers. She had enormous charm, vivacity and showed an ingenuity born of the desperate situations in which the brothers were continually finding themselves.

Basking in the glamour of appearing in uniform on 24 hours special leave, Grossmith attended the first night. And what a night. From the moment the curtain went up it was clear the show was a hit. At the end, when Grossmith was taking a curtain call, the adoration of the audience was expressed as one uninhibited lady clambered over the orchestra to kiss. him

There followed in February 1917 "The Bing Girls are There", book again by George Grossmith and Fred Thompson. Most of the music was by Nat D Ayer who launched another evergreen "Let the Great Big World Keep Turning". The emphasis was indeed upon the girls for George Robey and Alfred Lester had temporally bowed out to make room for Lorna and Toots Pounds. They left the male element to the gentle romantic Joe Coyne of "Merry Widow" fame. He was assisted by a still undiscovered and surprisingly acrobatic Laddie Cliff

The "Girls" were a success, but mostly because they were following in the wake of the Boys

Grossmith did not contribute to the next Alhambra revue. Instead Cosmo Gordon-Lennox came back to help C.M.S.McLellan, author of the musical "The Belle of New York". "Round the Map, a musical globe trot", opened in July 1917. Violet Loraine remained in the company and Alfred Lester made his return. A pearly King, tap dancing on a roof garden turned out to be an as yet unknown Jack Buchanan.

George Grossmith returned with Fred Thompson to re-assemble all three stars for "The Bing Boys of Broadway". It opened in February 1918. America having by this time entered the war, the audience were highly receptive to the New York setting. It included an excursion to the sparking department of Fords Motion City. An even faster thing in motion, however, was Violet Loraine's diamond garter. A thief fobbed it onto the innocent Oliver who handed it to the police who returned it to Violet Loraine. Then it went all the way round again, this time including George Robey who, for some inexplicable reason, was disguised as a Red Indian. This, he discovered meant that as a matter of protocol, he must drink firewater. It made all the feathers in his headdress spring into the upright position

After this, the Alhambra revues came to depend on either one or other of the stars. It was Violet Loraine who stayed on for "Eastward Ho" which opened in September 1919. It was written by the strangely disparate pair Oscar Asche, author of "Chu Chin Chow" and Dornford Yates author of the arch Berry novels. Between them they produced what was little more than a trip to Egypt. Under the spell of a ruined city, the tourists, including Ralph Lynn, joined in a treasure hunt.

By 1921 Violet Loraine had left and George Robey assumed responsibility for "Robey en Casserole". Officially it was called a "kaleidoscopic innovation". In practice, it was not particularly spectacular. Memorable items included Robey, complete with clay pipe, appearing as "Bubbles", the picture in the news since it had been bought by Pears Soap to be used as an advertisement.

Grossmith, though, had no part in these two revues. He had sensed a change. He abandoned the new Gaiety Theatre and the Empire. He now took over the Winter Garden Theatre and embarked on a new phase of musical comedy in his career.

ALBERT DE COURVILLE

Albert de Courville was essentially a gambler. He was not a compulsive gambler, but he bet heavily and could happily win or lose 20,000 pounds in a night. But he also knew when to stop. He had always had considerable luck and not just at roulette. His life was so streaked by chance that his venture into the world of theatre was simply one of his lucky runs.

He had been born into a wealthy family but had to start earning his living sooner and more urgently than had been expected. Before going into the theatre he had shown a degree of success as a journalist. Here too he proved to have luck - luck that was backed by a degree of courage. One night, working on "The Evening News", he looked into the office before going to the theatre. Instead he found himself on the Zebrugge night ferry following the ill fated journey of passengers wrecked twenty hours earlier. The storm had not abated so that they could not be rescued and were still clinging to the wreck for their lives.

When the survivors were eventually brought into the hospital, the press was kept away. But de Courville hid in a cupboard for four hours before emerging and pretending he was a hospital orderly. He was the only one to get an eyewitness story.

Another time he was sent to report on a mine fire at Courriers, when two thousand miners were trapped and burnt. The fire was still raging and only one man was allowed down. de Courville made out he was a medical student at Zurich University and persuaded the miner's delegate to take him down as his assistant. He crawled along the underground galleries passing corpses of men completely carbonated and shining black.

This luck did not desert him even when he was on his holidays. He was visiting Guatemala and nearly became involved in a presidential revolution. He had just left Messina on the eve of the great earthquake and so was first on the spot to file a report.

Yet his first attempt as a theatrical impresario was strangely inept. At the height of the Diablo hoop craze, he signed up the best exponent he could find. He then booked a London theatre and challenged anyone in the audience to come up and beat him. Unfortunately the first person to take up the challenger beat the so-called champion to an embarrassing degree. He produced "Othello" with a Sicilian cast, highly original but far from profitable. Then, with his usual good fortune, he met Sir Edward Moss who invited him to become his secretary and assistant for the Moss Empire chain. When Sir Edward was taken ill de Courville assumed responsibility for productions at the Hippodrome. Soon the staff were horrified at the enormous bills he was running up in preparation for his first revue. Fortunately Sir Edward gave his full backing

In his globe trotting, de Courville had taken due note of spectacular revue the world over. Besides the splendid productions of George Grossmith at the Empire he had seen the Folies Bergere in Paris and the Ziegfeld and Schubert shows in New York. Of them all, he felt it was America with the dawning era of jazz that held most promise. His formula was made up of topical variety, pantomime and sheer spectacle. And of all these ingredients, he gave priority to spectacle. In this he included the chorus Not only did he choose girls that were as beautiful as any in the Ziegfeld line but he trained them to a pitch whereby they could hold an entire scene without aid from the principals.

To, this he added style all his own. He wrote in his autobiography:

"I have always believed that every big revue should have at least four big full stage spectacular effects and that these effects should be developed in the course of a musical number - with the interpolation of incidental ballad, music or other items, such as speciality dancing - and then revert back to the original melody, which would be played and replayed until it became popular. In this manner, I could repeat the strain of an air a great number of times and unconsciously the audience would become familiar with the tune. So as not to bore them by a continuous repetition, which would become intolerable if something different did not happen on stage on each repetition, I used always to begin these scenes with a definite set picture and develop it into two or sometimes three or more climaxes. This could be done either by a change in the scenery, in the lighting or by bringing on new sets of girls in different costumes and groupings. I always utilised certain trick properties or accessories, such as convertible parasols, which the girls would use at a particular moment, and generally work for an ever changing panorama, the whole scene sometimes lasting as long as eight or ten minutes"

For all his undoubted skill at spectacle, de Courville could also show complete blind spots over good taste. In one production he starred a dancer who obviously had very little ability. His real reason was that she was the wife of a sensational murderer shortly to be hanged. Then, as though trying to redeem such lapses, he would commission a prestigious author to write a sketch and then, perversely, present it anonymously. He did this with E.V.Lucas, ascribing the work to a fictitious F.M.Mark and when he persuaded J.M.Barrie to write a sketch "The Dramatists Get What they Want" he had the authorship kept a closely guarded secret.

The title of his first Hippodrome revue conformed to his American bias: "Hello Ragtime" opened just before Christmas 1912. The title was by no means the only thing American. All the principals were American with the exception of Bransby Williams and he felt so out of place he left even before the first night. There was an American ragtime octet made up of the rough and ready types whom New York music publishers used to promote their songs in the Coney island cafes. Transplanted on to the Hippodrome stage, dressed in tails and sitting on little gilt chairs, they obviously felt as out of place as had Bransby Williams.

All the big numbers were sung by American rag time stars. The first London renditions of "Everybody's Doin' It" and "Alexander's Rag Time Band" were by Maud Tiffany, a sensational debut in what transpired to be a meteoric career dramatically cut short. Other notable songs in the production were "Waiting for the Robert E Lee" and "Hitchy Koo" sung by Lew Hearne and Bonita, sitting at a refreshment table at the White City Exhibition.

Moris Harvey also joined the Hippodrome company

Ethel Levy was the ideal singer of ragtime. Her voice ranged from basso profundo upwards and was permeated with a perfect sense of rhythm. Maybe her profile was not all that prepossessing but she had irrepressible energy. She would strut on to the stage with her sprightly, birdlike feet and go straightway into a routine of high kicks. It was she who evolved the ragtime singer's gesture on reaching the climax of holding arms outstretched.

Then there was Shirley Kellogg. She was not so much conventionally pretty as handsome, coupled with a magnetic stage presence. Her attributes were ideal for a large theatre, strengthened with a strong voice. She had a penchant for the gangway which helped her quickly establish an easy relationship with the audience. She later became Mrs. de Courville.

*Early audience participation. Shirley Kellogg leads the chorus along the joy plank
at the Hippodrome.*

"Hullo Ragtime" was so successful it ran to a second edition. This included the song "Get out and Get Under", when the girl being taken "for a spin" found the car would break down every time her boyfriend was about to kiss her.

Altogether "Hullo Ragtime" lasted almost a year, in those days a very successful run.

de Courville's second revue had much less American influence and was more international. There was a touch of the Gallic for the tango was the rage of Paris and the title was "Hello Tango". Russian influence was there too for Leon Bakst designed the beautiful costumes, "and so they ought to be" de Courville remarked "at the cost of 50 pounds per design". The American influence was further diluted since Shirley Kellogg was not in the show.

Ethel Levy remained to represent the USA and sang "Some of these Days", her last appearance before moving over to the Empire. The essentially English Violet Loraine was the other vocalist. She had been discovered by de Courville touring the provinces. She had always been the soubrette and was most dubious when de Courville insisted she should try her hand at comedy. However her immediate and enormous success as a coster woman selling whelks and shrimps in Piccadilly while singing "Dear Old Saturday Night" fully convinced her he was right. Indeed it proved a turning point in her career for soon after she teamed up with George Robey in "The Bing Boys" series.

The cast also included Billy Merson, George Arthur and Jack Morrison who put over the tongue twister "Sister Susie Sewing Shirts for Soldiers".

Harry Tate was another successful discovery of de Courville's. He and his gang were an immediate success and stayed on at the Hippodrome for several shows. His series of sketches were always about some leisure activity such as gardening, golfing, flying, billiards and, of course, the most famous of all, motoring. He had a thick son who would sit in the back, wearing an Eton collar and top hat and making idiotic remarks in a high falsetto. So it was little wonder Harry would occasionally threaten to "whip him with barbed wire".

Came the First World War and failing to realise the genuine value of entertainment in raising morale, de Courville made the same mistake as all the other impresarios. He felt he should not indulge in anything frivolous or luxurious unless, of course, it expressed patriotism. He even applied this policy to the title "Business as Usual", which opened in November 1914. One scene depicted a cavalry charge. It was, in fact, a clever bit of staging, using revolving platforms to create a remarkable sense of speed. He also put in rather puerile jokes about the Kaiser. But laughs and enthusiasm only changed from the semi-dutiful into the spontaneous when Harry Tate tried to catch pigeons in Trafalgar Square convinced they were all carrying messages to the Germans.

Morris Harvey left to join the banner of C.B.Cochran. de Courville brought in Herman Darewski, a proven and prolific composer

de Courville's next revue opened in May 1915 and was called "Push and Go". By this time, London had settled down to a more purposeful if less self conscious routine of wartime life. So there was a return to pre-war frivolity. Harry Tate tried to sell his "Rolls-Ford" and a mighty peculiar car it looked too. The dances were becoming almost tortuous with the steps of the "Tangle Foot Monkey Wrench".

"Joyland" opened there in December 1915. An undistinguished score was redeemed by even greater spectacle than usual There was a full sized landing stage lavishly decked with flags and a liner in the background. Drummers marched along the footlights while Bertram Wallis sang "The Flag Song". But even better was "Tulip Time", one of de Courville's most memorable effects. The main sequence depended on a hundred girls each bringing on and setting down four tulips. With four hundred flowers on stage, the whole depended on precise positioning to allow room for children to perform a tulip dance finale.

As so often happens when spectacle becomes the main attraction, the principals find they have little to do. There was the French dancer Yeetta Riangna. Shirley Kellogg spent even more time than usual down amongst the audience. Besides Bertram Wallis, there was another male newcomer, John Humphries.

"Flying Colours" opened at the Hippodrome in September 1916. The title was about the only item in the revue that could be associated with wartime. There was an indirect reference through a skit on the way West End managements were playing safe by reviving vintage musicals. Nothing less than "The Merry Chocolate Bell of the Mountains" could adequately summarise the full depths of degradation. Then there was a "Bairnsfatherland" sketch based on the inimitable sketches of the great cartoonist of the trenches - a prelude to C.B.Cochran's full length musical "The Better 'Ole". "A Dancing Carnival" self consciously illustrated types of dance from Ancient Greece down to the notorious Paris Tango. The quaisi Spanish dance was entrusted to Little Titch in skirts. Others in the cast besides Bertram Wallis and John Humphries included Gabrielle Ray from the Daly musicals and Dorothy Ward soon to make her name as pantomime's supreme principal boy.

At the same time Wal Pink - furious if anyone ever dared call him Walter - was brought in by de Courville as a permanent addition to his staff. Pink's intuition over an audience's response was so acute he could work any situation and be sure of raising a laugh precisely as required. Further more he could take somebody's suggestion, however vague, and work it into a certain success.

It was also in 1916 that de Courville had one of his occasional forays at a different theatre. In June he took over Drury Lane to present "Razzle Dazzle". For some time he had been hankering to produce a spectacular show in a fully equipped theatre.

Seizing his chance, he engaged a cast of 300 who seemed to be in a continual state of walking on. They processed across in a banqueting scene and, in true de Courville style they were outrageously dressed to represent some dish. There was caviar, lobster salad, pheasant, champagne and as chef d'euvre, Phyllis Bedells appeared as ice cream. The chorus were appropriately grouped for tableaux of Drake and Nelson at their most glorious moments. Such a theme had, of course to be brought up to date. So there were battleships and dreadnaughts while up front was Harry Dearth singing "England Remember". Mindful that there were other regions of the United Kingdom, the first half closed with Harry Dearth singing "Scotland for Ever". Set on a hillside, de Courville brought on what he considered the necessary quantity of girls in line formation. Each line was dressed in a different tartan. They were followed by a band of Scottish pipers and sword dancers. de Courville made the climax a complete contrast. A gillie led on stage a little boy in kilts set on a pony. After all the hundreds of girls, he certainly achieved the contrast he was seeking.

The enormous company were kept no less busy in the second half. It opened with "Maid of the Mist" which told the supposed legend of the yearly sacrifice of a native girl to the spirit of the Niagara Falls. Then in "A Modern Revue". the backdrop showed the auditorium complete with stage boxes and first two rows of stalls. Those appearing on stage played the scene with their backs to the real audience. The grand finale was "Skating at St.Moritz" with a piece of real ice providing a minuscule skating rink.

Such spectacle reduced the choice of principal to those few heavyweight players able to dominate a large audience. de Courville had in fact built the piece round George Robey but he was taken ill. So he was fortunate in signing up Harry Tate again, one of the few suitable replacements.

Altogether nothing was too big for this show - except the overheads. Fortunately its popularity proved as big as the production. So when the opportunity arose, de Courville transferred "Razzle Dazzle" to the Empire, with its far larger auditorium. It enabled the production to move into profit and complete a run of 400 performances.

de Courville was simultaneously preparing another show for the Hippodrome. He called it "Zig Zag" and it opened in January, 1917. It proved amazingly sumptuous even by de Courville standards.

He happened to hear one of the chorus girls whistling. Struck by her dexterity he incorporated her into the show. Then, during a motoring trip he had been struck by a view from the edge of a wood with a lake in the distance. He brought all this together to form the highlight of the production. The curtain rose to show the corner of the wood, almost neutral with the trees and falling leaves predominantly in ochre. The chorus girl walked across the stage, whistling a refrain. She was followed by Winnie Melville now singing the words "When Autumn Leaves are Falling". Then what had hitherto seemed to be piles of leaves, stirred into life and materialised as girls. By this time the full orchestra had taken up the melody and the girls danced their way off. The falling leaves had now turned to orange and next heaps of orange leaves stirred, came to life and the girls danced off. This theme was repeated in lemon and finally gold. Then the girl, still whistling the same song, crossed the empty stage again as the curtain fell.

The extraordinary facility of George Robey in having complete control of the audience was shown on the first night. He was supposed to be an inebriated gentleman who had booked a box in the Savoy theatre in mistake for a room at the hotel. He was convinced the programme girl was the chambermaid. Robey soon realised the audience was not fully responding. So almost imperceptibly, he changed from being an inebriated gentleman into a naive Yorkshire man. It did the trick. The laughs began coming faster and it ended as one of the most successful sketches of the evening. Robey also played an operatic barber, the sketch ending with him and his customer discussing the subtle flavour of the soap. He burlesqued the vogue for quick change artistes. He emerged from behind a screen as Doris Keen in "Romance" who " just wants to be good". He went on to appear first on one side of the screen and then on the other with ever increasing speed as her husband, her lover, the butler and Signor Poperinello, "de great dete-c-a-tif" from Scotland Yard.

Robey then appeared in a Stonehenge version of the eternal triangle. He informed the audience from behind an array of bristles surrounding his chin that he was Mr. Stonehatchet or he of the auburn locks. Daphne Pollock was Mrs. Stonehatchet or she of the tireless tongue. She, in turn made love to George Clarke, or he of the knotted knees.

In truly romantic vein, Daphne Pollock was a girl lost in a maze singing for someone to help find her way out. Other songs in the show included "Over There" sung by Shirley Kellogg while Cicely Debenham, as Little Miss Shy Lamb sang over the telephone to Bertram Wallis, her soldier boyfriend in France. With "Zig Zag", Albert de Courville received the compliment of being the only British producer to have his revue reproduced in its entirety at the Folies Bergere.

In the absence of George Robey, Harry Tate assumed responsibility for the comedy in "Box o' Tricks" which opened in March 1918. Among other guises, he appeared as the leader of a ladies orchestra, playing a trombone which inconveniently expanded across Cicely Debenham, earnestly playing the double base. He also appeared as a ship's passenger in continual fear of being torpedoed and driven frantic by the incessant popping of champagne corks. This time the customary " stunt" chorus number had the girls carrying out evolutions called out by a man in the audience.

For the opening procession in the next revue "Joy Bells" the chorus was decked out as tropical birds. George Robey was back but even he seemed somewhat subdued under the massed spectacle. He was partnered by Phyllis Bedells, her last show with de Courville

In December de Courville put "Joy Bells" into a second edition. He kept the opening scene with the tropical birds and introduced a winter scene which was suddenly transformed into spring. But most of the new edition comprised simple sketches. They included another example of his strange lapses in taste. This time it was a chorus of demobilised officers who were unemployed at a time when unemployment was something to be ashamed of. The stunt was all the more embarrassing since the programme gave their substantive ranks.

George Robey appeared as a father who had somehow missed out on war time lingo and was completely mystified as his children talked about tanks, over the top and Big Bertha. In "No, No, No" he turned lines that would normally seem perfectly ordinary into something highly suggestive. Daphne Pollock was a harassed maid of all work, falling off the ladder whilst cleaning windows, "though there's nothing to show for it all". Another sketch added to the second edition was "The Rest Cure" when an invalid is visited by friends on the eve of his operation. They describe the awful things that have happened to their friends under similar circumstances. The final visitor cheerily points out that if all does not go well then "I'll be seeing you - even if you don't see me."

"Jig Saw", de Courville's next Hippodrome show, opened in June 1920. It starred the Dolly Sisters who made a big hit with their Pony Trot. Winnie Melville sang "Kandy Kisses" and Stanley Lupino and Laddie Cliff started what was to become a long term partnership, as two scene shifters at the stage door, making pertinent comments on people and affairs. This was de Courville's last revue at the Hippodrome. In 1923 he produce a revue by George Gershwin called "The Rainbow" at the Empire.

There followed three shows at another of the Moss Empire theatres, the Palladium. The first "Whirl of the World" opened in March 1924. It was an example of de Courville at his most lavish; so lavish, in fact, one critic had the sensation the chorus girls were only appearing during the odd moments they could spare between changing costumes. The climax to the first half had Ethel Hook mounting steps reaching from the footlights right up into the flies. As she mounted so her crimson velvet cloak spread wider and wider until it covered the whole flight of stairs.

The Queens famous miniature dolls house was blown up to life size. The sides opened to reveal Myrro and Natove doing a semi nude acrobatic dance. They were immediately followed by Nervo and Knox burlesquing them and gradually changing the dance until it became a spoof slow motion wrestling match. A third comedian, Billy Merson appeared in a wild west courtroom sketch where he shot everyone daring to give evidence against him. Finally in a burlesque of "Hassan" Nellie Wallace appeared as a highly provocative Yasmin dancing in a rather peculiar yashmak.

de Courville gave "The World" a second whirl, though without Nellie Wallace. Instead the chorus did the Wiggle Waggle Walk which was not nearly so good. Billy Merson sang "What could be fairer than that" with Peter Bernard and Charles Austin barracking from the stage box.

And finally de Courville produced "Sky High" which opened in March 1925. Nellie Wallace returned and together with Arthur Riscoe burlesqued June and Jack Buchanan.

Typical of the no-expense-spared style of Albert de Courville is this fabulous chorus number in "Sky High" in 1925

Like journalism, the theatre was to prove no more than an interlude in de Courville's life. Of course it was a major interlude and, as things worked out, his greatest interlude. He then followed the logical path and went into films. He aped the Hollywood moguls and started behaving in an extraordinary manner. He signed up Jessie Matthews and then kept her on set in full make up for a week without using her. Cicely Courtneidge also experienced some of his erratic ways. "He directed me in a circus film. Now I can ride a pony but naturally I have not tried hand stands in Hyde Park on my morning canters". de Courville got impatient and brought in the reputed " Queen of the Circus" to show how it should be done - she was carried off on a stretcher. On another occasion de Courville thought it would make a good close up shot if Cicely was hit in the face by a tennis ball. Fortunately his boss, Michael Balcon, learnt about it just in time. So it was hardly surprising that he suffered a nervous breakdown and it is doubtful if he ever recovered. He spent much of his latter years in New York, responsible for occasional productions, most of them straight and none of them notable. The exception was the westernisation of a Chinese play "Lute Song".

ALFRED BUTT

Grossmith and de Courville had come upon spectacular revues through a world knowledge of show business. They also had an implicit feeling for what the public wanted. The third major producer of early spectacular revue, Alfred Butt, combined a limited knowledge of show business with an intimate knowledge of accountancy. His conventional career had started as an accountant at Harrods. One of his superiors recommended him to Charles Moreton, manager of the Palace Theatre while it was still playing variety. Moreton thought so much of the young accountant that on his retirement he recommended him as his successor. Alfred Butt also had the advantage of South African diamond millionaire Solly Joel as an angel. He worked on the principle that it is economic to pay stars whatever money they wanted so long as they, in turn, attracted the public in sufficient numbers to show a profit. Lady Constance Stewart Richardson was not particularly renowned for her dancing skills. Yet the distinction of her title and her place in society, coupled with the fact she was quite prepared to dance in diaphanous dresses, made her worth every penny of 350 pounds a week. 750 pounds seemed good value to tempt George Alexander and Beerbohm Tree to descend from the clouds of the classics to vulgar variety.

As a result the shareholders enjoyed a regular and satisfactory 20,000 pounds annual profit. Even when Butt strayed from his well proved formula, his flair for show business brought him success. He wanted to stage a musical "Going Up" but the rights were tied in with another piece. He bought the package. Not only did "Going Up" run for over 500 performances but the obligatory part of the deal turned out to be the enormously successful " Lilac Domino".

After five years staging variety Butt decided to join in the vogue for spectacular revue. By 1914 Grossmith and de Courville had, between them, all successful revue artistes under contract. So Butt set out to find his own. As before he paid good money for first class talent.

His first production "The Passing Show" which opened in April 1914 was full of talent. He brought Elsie Janis over from America. She was such an unknown quantity in London the accountancy in him came to the fore. He refused to pay the equal to her American salary until she had actually proved her worth with the Palace audiences. There need have been no question. From the moment during her first song when she started letting her hair down, scattering the stage with hairpins, the audience was her slave. Butt had played safe and had also signed up Gwendoline Brogden who had already made her name in musicals. One of her songs was "On Sunday I walk Out with a Soldier". It had not been particularly successful when the show opened and it was still peace time. On the declaration of war two months later it enjoyed enormous popularity as a recruiting song. Basil Hallam sang "Gilbert the Filbert" until he left to join the Army. He was killed in action. Also there was "Bunch" Nelson Keyes. He had made his name in "The Arcadians" and this was his first time in revue. It was to become his metier.

As he came on stage the first impression was of a dapper little man. He made full use of every facility. He had developed his facial muscle to the extent he could not only alter his expression but the actual shape of his face. Barely five foot two, he still could appear several inches taller. He helped achieve this through material means. By assuming the average man is five foot nine, he had everything he wore, from the size of the buttons to the width of his tie, scaled down proportionately. It worked for he really could look seven inches taller. He would build up the character gradually and subtly but with a sure touch. By the end of the sketch the audience was convinced he was both mentally and physically that person. It was only when seeing his next character that it became possible to gauge the full extent of his versatility. He was highly strung

MR. COOK as Lamplighter.

BASIL: "Tell me, why do you darken the top of the lamp?"

LAMPLIGHTER: "In case of a Zeppelin raid."

BASIL: "If I were you I'd darken the bottom as well."

LAMPLIGHTER: "What for?"

BASIL: "In case of a submarine raid."

MR. MORRISON as Basil Hallam.

A dutiful patriotic first World War joke in 0564 Gerrard.

and moody and was not in the least concerned over whom he offended in private or with his impersonations.

To back this strong company, Butt built up a team of writers and composers. He had no trouble over choosing the chief contributor to the score. Herman Finck had been conductor of the Palace orchestra for more than twenty years. He had proven melodious versatility, providing tunes befitting whatever situation arose. Some, notably "In The Shadows" had proved major hits in their own right.

Arthur Wimperis was made resident author. His school had been musical comedy for he had written "The Gay Gordons", "The Balkan Princess" and, above all "The Arcadians". He had already veered towards revue having contributed a number of sketches to "The Follies" seaside pierot show which had become a freak West End success. He was adept at translating sketches from the French, retaining the caustic Parisian wit yet avoiding the commonplace which can so easily creep in during translation. He had initially been an artist which may have been why his sketches so often depended on the visual for their effect.

A year later Butt introduced a new edition. With an accountant's impeccable logic he called it "The Passing Show 1915". He retained his principal composer Herman Finck and the stars Nelson Keyes, and Gwendoline Brogden. He introduced a delicate dancer who called herself simply June. This was quite understandable since her surname, before she became Lady Inverclide, was Tripp.

Now that it was clear the war would not be over by Christmas, Wimperis avoided the mistake of jeering at Gerry and bludgeoning the audience with patriotism. The few reference to hostilities were made with real wit rather than jingoism. Of course there were lapses as when Nelson, as Herman and Gwendoline as Gretchen sang "Got bless Old England" declaring "Britain is so delightful a residence for enemy aliens". A complete fallacy at a time when crowds were smashing the window of any shops with anything approaching a German name on the front.

Nelson Keyes also played a prominent part - or rather parts - in a skit on "David Copperfield". He appeared as a highly unconvincing Little Emma and proceeded to sing the contents of her letter to a far from handsome Ham. It says much for his skill that he still raised a laugh from such debased Dickens lines as "Your face will haunt me as long as I live. What a pity we can't hit it off". His chances were improved as he also played Uriah Heep. In another sketch Keyes appeared as one of the growing band of reckless drivers. He recognised only two types of pedestrian: the quick and the dead.

Butt followed this in September with "Bric a Brac". He provided each contributor with an assistant. Arthur Wimperis was helped by Basil Hood, also of musical comedy fame. Herman Finck was assisted by Lionel Monckton of The Gaiety. Glamour was added in the form of Gertie Millar.

One of the highlights of "Bric a Brac" was the diminutive Nelson Keyes alongside the tall and languid Arthur Playfair. They were guardsmen on sentry duty outside St.James's Palace. They emerged from their respective sentry boxes to peruse the paper and, as "The Optimist and the Pessimist" sing their pertinent comments.

The vogue for everything Russian, riding on the back of the success of the Diagelev ballet, produced two appropriate numbers for Gertie Millar: "Salade Russe" and "Peter from Petrograd". Teddie Gerrard maintained the theme with "Olga from the Volga". She won by far her greatest reception in "Oh, Naughty Naughty One Gerrard". Everyone in the audience knew she had just been jilted by the young Peter Robinson and that the telephone number of his father's Oxford Street store was Gerrard 0001.

Butt staged "Vanity Fair" in November 1916. Up to now his revues had been relatively modest. Now he felt sufficiently confident to rival the capital outlay so lavishly dispersed by de Courville. He had a de Courville type extravaganza ballet called "The Romance of the Dragonfly". Another sketch was extraordinary for the set was entirely black with the principals dressed as lumps of coal. Contrast came with the chorus, dressed in silver. Even the musical chosen for the inevitable burlesque was the most sumptuous then to be seen in London "Chu Chin Chow".

Butt's next revue at the Palace was "Airs and Graces" which opened in June 1917. This time he made major changes in both staff and cast. Arthur Wimperis left to join Andre Charlot and Nelson Keyes for de Courville. Herman Finck, still loyally in the orchestra pit, wrote the score with Lionel Monckton giving strong support. Monckton had now married his Gaiety colleague, Gertie Millar. It was rumoured she had engineered it as she wanted to ensure having all the best tunes. The company were first seen in a charming stretch of countryside. Gertie Millar appeared as a lady of title equipped with a vast quantity of agricultural implements and a determination to "do her bit". She was soon joined by a no less fetching group of land girls, led by Gracie Leigh. They were supervised by three gentlemen, led by John Humphries, sent down by the Bureau of National Service. However rural the pleasures might be, they were considered insufficient on their own. Soon Gertie Millar, who had no pretensions over her background as a former Lancashire mill hand, was leading a chorus of Lancashire mill lasses, complete with shawls and clogs, in a waltz "Ding a Ding". Then she appeared perched amid roof tops with the chorus dressed as chimney sweeps and pussy cats. John Humphries, too, had his moments notably as a comedian in an ancient Assyrian music hall, desperately trying to be funny against the knowledge that failure meant he would be thrown to the lions.

Butt's tendency to copy the de Courville formula became even more evident with the title of his next revue "Hullo America". Its claim to topicality lay with America's entry into the war. Elsie Janis led the chorus in dresses incorporating sections of the stars and stripes. At the climax, she would open the flaps of her coat to reveal the U.S.Flag in its entirety. Later she rose like Venus - but out of a large basket labelled Y M C A.

America was further represented by Jerome Kern. His nostalgic song "They'll Never Believe Me" had already swept the country. Lloyd George said he would rather have written it than be Prime Minister. So now, here in person on the Palace Stage, Kern was singing his new composition "The Picture I want To See". More in accordance with his usual self , Butt had also signed up the leading matinee idol of the straight theatre Owen Nares.

Then there was Stanley Lupino, initiating the audience into the dubious ways whereby anyone who had lost their meat ration coupons could avail themselves of someone else's book. In the second edition, which opened in February 1919, Stanley Lupino was replaced by Billy Merson and Owen Nares by a young Frenchman who created a sensation on the first night: Maurice Chevalier.

Finally Butt acquired an actual de Courville revue; "The Whirlgig". But the Palace did not have the same atmosphere as the Hippodrome. Besides "Whirlgig" depended essentially on one person, Masie Gay. While she was extremely good, particularly as Mrs. Harris in a sketch by Edgar Wallace, even she could not save the piece on her own.

The years of revue at the Palace ended when Alfred Butt, soon to become Sir Alfred, moved over to manage Drury Lane. There he specialised in American musicals, especially the spectacular ones which, it was hoped, would counteract the growing threat of "the talkies"

To start with Butt continued his policy of paying large salaries to attract major stars. But they were American stars and he soon realised that on their own they did not even fill a row of stalls. He then fell into financial trouble, made worse through being involved in the scandal surrounding the financier J.H.Thomas.

CHAPTER III
INTIMATE REVUE

Intimate revue, like spectacular revue, started in Paris, though it was much earlier than in England - in 1640 to be precise. It did not, however, reach London for another two centuries. The reason was largely one of censorship. The French considered it perfectly normal for government leaders to have a mistress and the rest of society did the same. So there was no censor to hamper what often amounted to scurrilous satire.

In England, however, censorship had been imposed by Walpole, prime minister in a government so riddled with corruption it could not withstand criticism. So when revue eventually reached London, the Lord Chamberlain hobbled the enterprise and for the next century fiercely shielded thin skinned politicians .

The cat and mouse game of trying to get material past the Lord Chamberlain became an involved matter. In 1873 he had ruled out a skit on Gladstone and three of his colleagues in "Happy Land" at the Royal Court. It was certainly spiced for it was by a certain W.S.Gilbert in the days before he had met Sullivan. In 1903 when "The Linkman", was staged at the old Gaiety, the censor evidently failed to appreciate the degree of wizardry made possible by the recent development of grease based make-up. He passed the apparently innocent script only to be startled in performance to see four of the cast as the spitting image of Lloyd George, George Bannerman, Balfour and Joseph Chamberlain, unmistakable with his eyeglass and an orchid in his buttonhole. Partly because it was a fait accompli and partly because of the short run scheduled, he was, with difficulty, persuaded to let it be.

Perversely, the Lord Chamberlain had no powers of censorship if the performance did not last longer than half an hour. This put it in the same category as public house entertainment. So it was this ruling that allowed the impersonation of Asquith, Lloyd George and McKenna in a good natured skit in an Alhambra revue in 1905

By and large, though, authors had to turn to fellow thespians and others in the arts for their targets, confident they would not spoil a colleague's fun.

French "revue" was aptly named for it usually reviewed, in a witty and often cruel way, the political and social events of the past season. To start with they were tacked on to existing productions at the end of the season. It was a way of persuading audiences to see the show for a second time.

In its early days, English revue retained the traditional French format with a compère and commère. One was a sophisticated, blasé man about town. The other was a naive boy or girl up from the country now that the Season was over. They would be introduced to one another and the compère would offer to show the commère around the city making witty and pungent comments. In France the two never actually left the stage but would drift to either side of the proscenium to make way for the next song or sketch.

The idea was not completely foreign to London for traditionally the music hall had always had a master of ceremonies to introduce the various turns. The difference between music hall, and variety was that while both were made up of individual turns, revue had a cast who would appear under different guises throughout the evening.

The first revue in London was a "one off" written by an author who had learnt his trade in burlesque. "Success, or a Hit if You Like" was put on at the Adelphi in 1825. It was written by J.R.Planche who's puns were outrageous even for burlesque. However his essay into the revue was marred by Lady Success, the daughter of Fashion. Far from being a success she merely restricted the proceedings through being the only woman in the piece.

Forty years separated this from the next revue "Sensations of the Past Season" which opened at the St.James's in 1863. This time the author straying from burlesque was H.J.Byron.

But the acceptance of revue as a form of theatre followed exactly the same lines as musical comedy. It was born to replace burlesque

The idea that revue could be a substitute had been canvassed by several actor authors. The first was Charles Brookfield, who wrote and appeared in "The Poet and the Puppets" at the Comedy in May 1892. However it suffered from the same shortcomings as had beset Lady Success. This time, though, it was a man. Certainly anyone prepared to walk down Piccadilly in velvet pantaloons contemplating the beauty of a lily held in his hand qualified as a satisfactory subject for satire. Gilbert had found it so in "Patience". But Brookfield, it soon became clear, had an obsession over Oscar Wilde. But no one, no matter how colourful, is sufficient material for a complete evening's entertainment.

A year later Brookfield teamed up with another actor/author, Seymour Hicks and together they wrote and appeared in "Under the Clock" at the Court Theatre in 1893. They provided an amusing super sleuth Sherlock Holmes as compère with a distinctly dim Dr.Watson as commère. This time, with the assistance of Lottie Venne and Robert Nainby, they spread the satire more evenly. They impersonated Herbert Beerbohm Tree, Wilson Barrett, Henry Irving, Julia Neilson and Mrs. Patrick Campbell as "The Third Mrs. Tanqueray" staggering about the room murmuring "I can't go straight - I can't go straight". But no matter how various the impersonations nor how ingeniously depicted, when seen in quantity, the evening became monotonous.

The next revue was "Pot Pourri" which opened at the Avenue in 1899. It was written by James Tanner who incorporated all the usual theatrical gossip. He gave it a degree of unity by providing a plot that was in itself a skit on the outrageous Drury Lane melodramas. Examples of disasters that had overtaken hero or heroine in recent years had included a heroine cast adrift in a balloon only to find her companion was an escaped lunatic; a hero and villain locked in desperate conflict - in diving suits on the sea bed!

Upon this ridiculous framework Tanner superimposed a satirical view of several other current West End successes including J.M.Barrie's "The Little Minister" and Pinero's "The Gay Lord Quex". There were also impersonations of Charles Hawtrey as Lord Algy, of Edna May as a Salvation Lassie even more demure than she was in "The Belle of New York", a sickly sweet Ellaline Terriss in "The Shop Girl" and Marie Tempest, recently sacked from the cast of "The Geisha" for cutting her Japanese trousers into shorts.

So it was no great leap forward when, towards the end of 1903 Tanner adapted the idea for the few final performances before the Gaiety Theatre was due to be pulled down. As a "souvenir",

Tanner together with the junior lead George Grossmith, devised a tribute to all the past shows. He called it "The Linkman", the man who called the carriages for members of the audience leaving after the play. Just as in Paris, "The Linkman" was tacked on to the end of the current musical "The Toreador".

It had the advantage that the company were already well known and loved by the audience. Much of the delight came from recognising Robert Nainby as the stage door keeper and Connie Ediss as the wardrobe mistress.

But it was George Grossmith, no doubt encouraged by his success with "The Linkman", who realised that revue could be sufficiently popular to be made a major item on the bill. On leaving The Gaiety he assumed responsibility for the shows at The Empire. It was a large auditorium to fill so after one or two small productions , he concentrated on spectacle. This left a complete absence of intimate revue in the London theatre until the arrival of C.B.Cochran in 1914.

C.B.COCHRAN

Cochran had the facility, as did George Edwardes, of producing a success which still failed to pay its way. But, as with Edwardes, it is unfair to use the number of performances as a criterion to any of his productions. Many were of the highest calibre but did not prove a success commercially.

Indeed, Cochran had many things in common with Edwardes, though not necessarily so unfortunate. They both liked to be in at the very beginning of an idea for a show. Then they could guide and mould its growth up to and after the first night. They both had an intuitive understanding of the various aspects of production and insisted on everything being of the best quality.

Before arriving in the West End, Cochran had promoted circuses, roller skating and boxing matches. So it is strange that after such various and sensational ventures, he chose to make his theatre debut in intimate revue. Indeed his early shows were not only intimate but parsimonious. But he had his mind on quality. Before making up his mind, he discussed his ideas with Bernard Shaw and H.G.Wells. "Odds and Ends" opened at the Ambassadors Theatre in October, 1914. He took only too literally a remark made by Ernst Stern, the famous German director, that there is no problem in decor that cannot be solved with a little black velvet. The whole of "Odds and Ends" was played against black velvet drapes with the exception of the opening number. That was set on the bare stage. His authors made light of this parsimony in a programme note: "Mr. Cochran wishes to announce that he has spared no economy in mounting this revue".

Working to such limits, Cochran was relying heavily on the skill of both his authors and stars. They did not let him down. It was Harry Grattan's essay in revue but his work in the music hall had already proved him deft among writers. His very first revue sketch shoved he was no less adept at this new form. It was a skit on the current vogue for infant geniuses. The star was Alice Delysia who had been playing leading parts in Paris - but only as an understudy. She was ably supported by Leon Moreton. Douglas Furber, who is best remembered as a highly prolific lyrist, on this occasion played the lover.

The total effect was sheer audacity shot with the unconventional. The audience delighted in never being sure what might happen next.

Indeed the whole programme was curious for the revue made up only a third of the evening. It was the filling in a bizarre international sandwich. A Japanese one act play came before and a French one act piece came after.

Cochran's determination and self confidence was soon severely tested. The critics did not like "Odds and Ends". However with his experience Cochran was not prepared to let matters rest there. He immediately set about making drastic alterations - and they were the correct ones. He realised the weakest point lay with the two one act plays. So Harry Grattan had to expand the revue until it took up the whole evening. Only after the show had acquired a quantity of devotees did Cochran invite the press for a second time. He knew only too well how demoralising can be a solid phalanx of critics, self consciously refraining from applauding. So he scattered them among his genuinely enthusiastic patrons. His plan worked admirably. Infected by the palpable enjoyment surrounding them the critics were next day extolling sketches that a few weeks before they had been castigating.

After this successful piece of engineering Cochran staged "More Odds and Ends" though, colloquially it was known as "More". Opening at the Ambassadors in June 1915, the mixture was much as before. Music was by Edward Jones, words by Harry Grattan who urged the audience to be seated promptly by 8.30 since the plot ended at 8.25. Mindful of the shortcomings of the previous production, there was a burlesque Japanese melodrama. It had seven murders in each act and in the finale all those who had so far survived committed hari-kari. He also provided a Victorian melodrama played in mime. At the end, the audience was invited to guess what it was all about. The stars were again Alice Delysia and Leon Moreton, also to be seen as Puck with a band of fairies in rags and tatters unemployment having reached fairlyland.

Cochran put "More" into a second edition in December. One of the best new sketches showed an author becoming increasingly dismayed as the cast insisted on "improving" his play. But worse, some of them turned out to have a strong American bias. And finally some French actors weighted in with their Gallic suggestions.

Cochran provided a successor in "Pell Mell" in June 1916. Harry Grattan had moved over to be with Grossmith at the Empire. So Fred Thompson and Morris Harvey were brought in with Nat D Ayer providing the music. The result was, if anything, rather more sophisticated even if it seemed to lose some of its spontaneity.

Thompson continued with Grattan's programme notes. One made the interesting point that the revue would be just as coherent if played backwards. There was another skit on infant prodigies, with little Winnie announced as having played the part of Clarice Lovebond upwards of 20,000 times. Leon Moreton appeared as a stranger in London perplexed by the number of people who selected him when they wanted to ask the way. He was also a naughty sultan to Delysia's ravishing slave girl in a burlesque on "Chu Chin Chow". Then Delysia appeared as a fraginard, permitting , nay encouraging an elderly marquise to help put on her stockings. Other sketches included the composer Nat D Ayer as an office manager engaging Dorothy Minto which naturally led into a typewriter duet, while the rest of the staff formed a chorus. Other Dorothy Minto songs included "What did Cleopatra do to Make Mark Anthony Laugh?" and "Dear old Broadway"

There followed in April 1917, "One Hundred and Fifty Pounds" in which , as the title suggests, Cochran followed much the same line as before. A programme note offered an apology that "due to a scene put in at the last minute, Mr. Cochran has been compelled to exceed the original estimate by four pounds, fifteen shillings."

*Impresarios, clockwise from top left: George Edwardes, Andre Charlot,
Albert de Courville and C.B. Cochran*

The opening scene was a street in Baghdad "painted and repainted by Marc Henri". A programme note explained the action: "First of all some time is devoted to gaining the right atmosphere and a nifty bit of acting to give the latecomers a chance to find their seats. When the moment comes, the street scene is interrupted by the arrival of the English troops, whereupon the traditional merry peasants rush on stage singing the opening chorus". There followed a spy story, highly complex and incorporating skits on the choruses to be seen at the Alhambra, Palace, Hippodrome and even the Ambassador Theatres itself.

Alice Delysia was not in this revue for Cochran was including her in his plans for expansion at the Pavilion. He decided to go ahead with this transfer despite the fact "One Hundred and Fifty Pounds" was a failure.

CHAPTER IV
STAR MUSICALS

With George Edwardes's death, coming as it did, in the early months of the Great War, the world was hardly in a state to encourage new ideas over the development of musical comedy. Therefore, for the next decade musical comedy, like musical romance, continued along its well worn path. The major change was to place considerably more emphasis upon the comedian Whereas Teddy Payne had shared star billing with the leading lady, the Adelphi musicals in the early 'twenties were built up entirely around the personality of W.H.Berry. Advertisements on the sides of the buses had W.H.BERRY in letters two foot high and more and the name of the musical tucked away in the bottom corner.

George Grossmith sensed this trend. He was also the natural successor to the Guv'nor at The Gaiety. While he proved as adept as Edwardes in selecting pretty girls he was also astute in picking his comedian. He chose Leslie Henson

LESLIE HENSON

Leslie Henson's had started his career in the third, or "fit up" company touring the George Dance musicals. He never appeared in a flop. But his greatest asset was his face. James Agate described how "in moments of ecstasy he looks at you out of eyes like those of a moth which has eaten too much tapestry". Henson could perfectly register every thought and feeling passing through his mind - horror, dismay, alarm, hope, pleasure or sheer befuddlement, all in rapid succession. He excelled at mime. Anything that happened to be at hand seemed to inspire his imagination. With a minimum of effort, he could quickly turn a sofa into a punt or a bolster into a roll of material. Like Arthur Roberts, he made up a song actually on stage. He sang it with Davy Burnaby in "Yes Uncle". The dominant line was "Would you believe it?" and it was so popular on the first night it was encored and encored again. The lyrist had foreseen this and given them several extra verses. But the audience still demanded more. So Henson embarked on a spontaneous verse, making up the first half with Davy Burnaby supplying the second. Not only did the result rhyme perfectly but they maintained the scansion.

Otherwise the Gaiety cast included such old hands as Robert Nainby and, of course, George Grossmith.

Their first production was "Tonight's The Night" . Due to Kitchener's wartime threat to close the theatres, the Schubert Brothers in New York suggested that the whole production should first of all be staged on Broadway "just until the war is over".

When "Tonight's The Night" opened in America, the critics complained that it did not have enough pep. Grossmith took the criticism to heart. Then, when it finally opened in the West End in April, 1915, the London critics complained that it had too much pep.

The hit song was an interpolated number called "They didn't Believe Me" by a promising young American called Jerome Kern. Except for "Any Old Night", also by Jerome Kern, the music was by Paul Rubens and included "Please Don't Flirt with Me" and "I Could Love you". The book was by Fred Thompson. Arkay in "The Tatler" declared it was rather like a risqué French story told for the amusement of young children. Grossmith showed he had every intention of continuing the Guv'nor's well proven formula with the books as well as the company. The story was composed of several plots neatly dovetailed. Each one opened an opportunity to one or two members of the company.

In September 1916, Grossmith followed with "Theodore & Co". This time it really was adapted from the French. Jerome Kern was entrusted with a large part of the score, the rest being written by Ivor Novello. Leslie Henson consolidated his success and was given star billing. He went on to steal the notices from George Grossmith who, as usual, was playing the part of a dude peer.

In the true Gaiety fashion, Henson had been given only the barest outline of a part and had to work out all the gags himself.

After this Grossmith transferred his sphere of activity to The Prince of Wales Theatre, opening in December 1917 with "Yes Uncle". It had such catchy tunes by Nat D. Ayer that even a number with a title as daunting as "Widows are wonderful" still became a hit.

The leading lady had to declare she was off to buy some stuff for a petticoat. One evening Henson surprised her by seizing one of the bolster shaped sofa cushions. Pretending it was a roll of material, he unrolled it, caressed it, measured it and, all in imagination cut, off a length and wrapped it up. Then he wrote out a bill, sent it by an overhead wire to the cashier's box, with his eyes following its path somewhere round the front of the dress circle. He waited for the change to arrive back and gave it to the customer, finally bowing the lady off the stage. Like so many of his improvisations, it was such a success that it was kept in for the rest of the run.

After "Yes Uncle", Grossmith again temporally transferred his activities, this time to the Shaftesbury. The company was, however, deprived of Leslie Henson who had joined up in the Royal Flying Corps.

When he was eventually demobbed, George Grossmith made him star of a successful series of musicals at the Winter Garden Theatre.

The first was an adaptation of an American piece called "The Girl Behind the Gun". However Grossmith considered, quite rightly, that the British were sick and tired of guns. So he changed it to the more acceptable "Kissing Time". It opened in May 1919. P. G. Wodehouse wrote the lyrics. It showed him to be a skilful as well as witty lyrist, perfectly at home with triple rhymes such as the wicked satire about Newport hostesses in "Sally"..

"If a leader you'd be reckoned
You must never lose a second
As a hostess you must follow what is new;
Every day you'll keep your eye on
Any likely social lion
Find a fresh attraction ev'ry month or two.

Say a rising politician or a musician with ambition
Or a painter with an ultra modern style;
Or a lovely foreign lady
Who is picturesquely shady;
She will keep you in the limelight for a while.

Wodehouse may, on first thoughts, have been an exception in writing witty lyrics for musical comedy. Noël Coward, Harry Graham, A.P.Herbert and the other witty lyrists all wrote for musical romances, not musical comedy. In fact British borne Wodehouse was no exception. Along with another erstwhile British author, former architect Guy Bolton, he had developed a new type of musical, one of adult sophistication which became known in New York as the Princess musicals. They went far towards making musical comedy audiences actually use their intelligence. They were, according to P.G.Wodehouse, " farce-comedies which relied on situation and character for laughs instead of the clowning and cross talk with which the largest musicals filled in the gaps between the romantic scenes". In some ways they were similar to the Gaiety musicals with the interest spread between all the characters. They also developed an unusually slick technique in introducing songs into the dialogue.

It was only during their trans Atlantic crossing that these pieces acquired the true English musical comedy formula. Notably this meant building the comedy up until it was the leading role always, of course, backed by Leslie Henson's special brand of dialogue.

Grossmith had not appeared on stage for some time. Indeed, many people were under the impression that he had retired. So at 45 he was, naturally, rather apprehensive about taking the juvenile lead. But then he decided he was the only one suitable. He took the risk and got away with it.

Grossmith had converted the Winter Garden from the "Old Mogul" music hall. It was commonly considered to be on the wrong side of Drury Lane but the success of "Kissing Time" put it firmly on the map.

In September, 1920 there followed "A Night Out". In this piece, Grossmith reverted to his policy by adapting a French farce. So naturally it was about the usual complications in mistaken hotel rooms. At last Grossmith relinquished the juvenile lead. "A Night Out " ran for almost a year, as did all his next three productions.

"Sally", again by Guy Bolton, opened in the following September. It had originally been staged by Florence Ziegfeld in new York. The two most memorable points about "Sally" were Jerome Kern's first major score and Dorothy Dickson's first chance as an actress. Three hit tunes were "Look for the Silver Lining", "I'm but a Wild Wild Rose" and "The Little Church Round the Corner".

Dorothy Dickson only previous appearance in London had been as a dancer in one of C.B.Cochran's Pavilion revues. She had good looks and dancing ability but a small voice. What voice she did have had a certain flatness in tone which made it sound monotonous. Later it was to improve. But the contract for this show gave both Kern and Ziegfeld the power of veto. When Kern heard her sing, he wielded it. Naturally he was most concerned over the way his songs were sung. He did not have the experience of Grossmith who remembered how Edwardes had taken a chance with Joe Coyne in "The Merry Widow". He went on rehearsing her in secret. On the first night Dorothy Dickson was an enormous success and Kern had to admit he had completely misjudged her.

For some time Grossmith had been wanting to form a Winter Garden quartet on the lines of Teddy Payne with Connie Ediss and Gertie Millar and himself at the old Gaiety. By public demand, Grossmith had now returned to play opposite Leslie Henson. Dorothy Dickson had agreed to stay on and the quartet was completed by Heather Thatcher, who Grossmith had discovered in "The Naughty Princess". Heather Thatcher was one of the few young and pretty leading ladies who did not care what she looked like so long as it was for the good of the piece. She could afford to do so for she had such a strong personality the audience always had her real self in mind, no matter how unbecoming her attire.

"Sally" gave an excellent opportunity for comparison between Grossmith's chorus girls and Ziegfeld's Follies. Grossmith's were, by common consent, declared to be the prettier. It was at about this time that C.B.Cochran caused a rumpus by saying that "even though English faces are just as pretty as American faces and even have more character, it is rare to find an English girl with the American good ankles and slim tapered legs". Two girls of the Winter Garden chorus at this time were soon to prove this. Winifred Shotter was to become a star in her own right, and Sylvia Hawkes accomplished the considerable feat of marrying two peers and two of Hollywood's top stars.

The Winter Garden chorus with George Grossmith, wearing morning coat,
Behind him, wearing cap is Leslie Henson.

It was chiefly through Grossmith that cabaret was first introduced into London. It was obviously a word the producers would be eager to incorporate in titles. So Grossmith jumped the gun and himself produced "The Cabaret Girl", a couple of months before the first cabaret opened in London at the Metropole Rooms. Unfortunately Leslie Henson fell ill just before the first night. After a short postponement, Norman Griffin was ready to fill the breach and it opened in September, 1922. This time the book was by Grossmith as well as P.G. Wodehouse. The music was again by Jerome Kern and included the song "Dancing Time". Leslie Henson, who was able to take over his part after the first few weeks, appeared in an assortment of disguises. They included a sporting parson, a Tyrolean mountaineer and a really clever impersonation of Gladys Cooper as the Second Mrs. Tanqueray.

"The Beauty Prize" followed in September, 1923. Again Leslie Henson added to the festivities. His antics included partnering Dorothy Dickson in three-legged and wheelbarrow races. The piece was further distinguished by its novel presentation of the chorus. They were dressed as winds, dragons, flower, circles etc all in deference to the fashionable game of Mah Jong:

> *"At all Swiss mountain resorts*
> *They've given up winter sports.*
> *They all stay indoors all day long*
> *And play Mah Jong.*

The creators of "The Beauty Prize" were again George Grossmith and P.G. Wodehouse whilst Jerome Kern was responsible for the music.

"Primrose" was produced in September the following year. Dorothy Dickson had left and Claude Hulbert arrived. The Grossmith-Bolton partnership produced a slap-dash story held together by taut dialogue. Every line was either working up to a comical situation or a song. The lively score introduced another composer from the New World, George Gershwin. His brother, Ira, wrote the lyrics. Henson sang a duet with Hulbert describing the awful things done to Mary Queen of Scots. Somehow, though, as through Chinese whispers, by the end of the song it had been churned it into "dairy cream in clots".

"Tell Me More" was produced in May 1925. Again the music was by George Gershwin, but the low comedy book tended to cancel out the sophisticated songs. For this production the company remained virtually unchanged. Leslie Henson sold hats. One of his customers found just the hat she wanted but it must be trimmed with a material to match the dress she was wearing. Henson said he had just the stuff. Retiring behind her he proceed to take snippets off the bottom of her skirt. Claude Hulbert distinguished himself by singing a duet with Vera Lennox all the time standing on his head.

In February 1926 there followed "Kid Boots". The title was not, as the London audiences then supposed, derived from some sort of footwear but was the American terminology for a shoe shine boy. He turned out to be Eddie Cantor on Broadway and Leslie Henson in London. Needless to say, Leslie Henson was again the backbone of the Winter Garden production. On this occasion, he was subjected to the indignity of being massaged by Diana Wilson. She pummelled him and finally put him into an electric chair for treatment. Also Claude Hulbert distinguished himself by devising and dancing an astonishing ballet. It depicted himself getting up, shaving, brushing his teeth and making general preparations for the day.

"Kid Boots" turned out to be the last production before the company was dispersed and George Grossmith really did retire.

W.H. BERRY

W.H. Berry had been principal comedian for Edwardes's productions at Dalys, notably in "The Merry Widow". But in this theatre where musicals were close to operetta he had always been fairly subdued. After Edwardes's death Berry felt he could not continue at Dalys any more. So he went over to the Adelphi and, for the first time shows were built entirely around the comedian.

W.H.Berry used to rely a good deal on props and no performance of his was complete without something outsize, vividly coloured or unexpectedly flexible. No matter what it was, his gusto and geniality always broke through to thaw even the most reticent audience. Behind lay an accomplished technique, for he took immense pains over detail. He had a neat sense of timing his retorts, which made him one of the few comedians in musical comedy who could get a belly laugh. After cracking a joke he had a habit of laughing himself and then kiss the nearest chorus girl, as though claiming a charming reward. He had a surprisingly good singing voice and, what is more, could sing off key to order, complexly shattering the composure of everyone on stage as well as in the audience. A heavily built man he was surprisingly light on his feet and tripping the light fantastic.

Berry opened in November, 1915 in "Tina". The odd title was due to a cocoa king, named Van Dam. He had a daughter, and since he had little thought for anything except business, he had christened her Cocoa Tina. However, for social purposes, it was abbreviated to just plain Tina. Van Dam was played by W.H.Berry, his daughter by Phyllis Dare. Godfrey Tearle was also in the cast, making one of his rare appearances in a musical. The music was by Paul Rubens and Hayden Wood It was a strange combination of talented amateur and, technically, a highly proficient musician. It resulted in quite a successful score including the songs "The Violin Song" and "I'm a Self Made Man".

It was followed in August 1916 by "High Jinks". It was the name of a magic perfume for everyone who smelt it immediately became agreeable. Adapted from the French by the highly experienced American Otto Harbach, it was further polished for the London production by the prolific comedy writer Frederick Lonsdale. It was set to music by another long experienced American Rudolph Friml. When it was staged in America, the greatest impact was made by the ladies in the cast. The British edition was greatly enhanced by Berry's interpretation of the part of Dr. Thorne. He turned it into one of the longest roles ever written in a musical comedy. He certainly proved himself for the piece ran for 383 performances. Typically Berry put a football bladder inside a sponge. When he angrily threw the sponge down, it would unexpectedly bounce back into his hands. Peter Gawthorne was also in the cast.

In September, 1917, came one of Berry's biggest successes "The Boy". Fred Thompson provided a close adaptation of Sir Arthur Pinero's play "The Magistrate". W.H.Berry was the magistrate Mr. Meebles. A straight-laced man, his son inveigles him into going to a disreputable night club. According almost to convention, his wife, unbeknown to him, also pays the club a visit - so do the police. Mr. Meebles managed to escape. As he was due to sit on the bench the next day and under the law of those times, he had to convict his wife, his son and their friends.

The part of the magistrate gave Berry a chance to show his real acting ability and it was one of his most successful parts. While he was dining at the night club first one of his son's lady friends and then another came up to talk. Each time, Berry dutifully stood up while they were chatting. Eventually, fearing his soup was growing cold, he removed a potted palm from off its stand. Still gripping it by the stalk, he put his plate on the stand and continued drinking his soup uninterrupted.

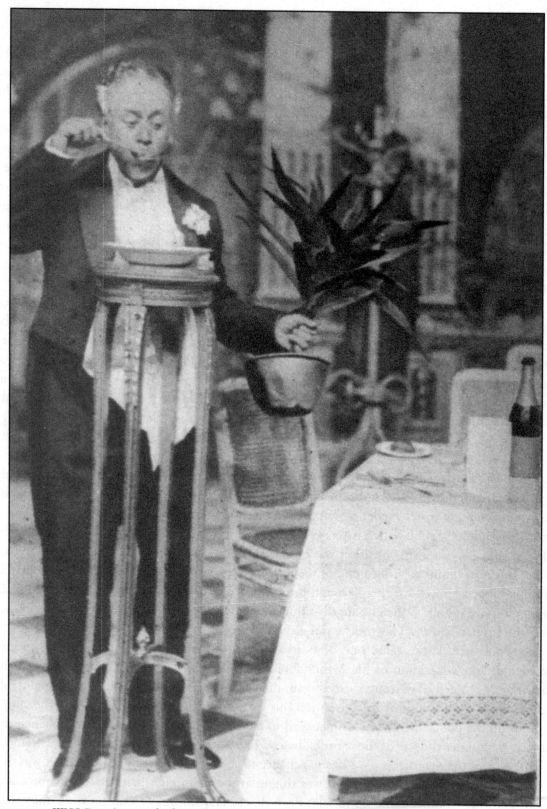

W.H.Berry's unorthodox solution to his soup growing cold in "The Boy" in 1917

Next morning he was seated at his desk in the magistrate's private room. During the run he discovered that if he stabbed his quill pen well down in the inkstand and let go suddenly it would fly up in the air. Turning with a quizzical expression he would ask: "Who's been filling this with India rubber ink?"

Once again the sub plot turned out to be equally amusing. A widow tries to encourage her admirer by declaring she is five years yonger than she really is. This was not appreciated by her son who according to this new calculation found he was in his early teens. This considerably diminished his eligibility in the eyes of his lady friends.

The music was by Lionel Monckton and Howard Talbot and was admirably in the spirit of the piece. Many considered it the best score Monckton ever wrote; it was also his last. It included "Little Miss Melody" and "I want to Go To Bye Byes".

"The Boy" was such a success it seemed only natural to follow it in September, 1919 with another Pinero adaptation. The play chosen was ""In Chancery" which for this occasion was renamed "Who's Hooper?" Vincent Hitchins loses his memory in a railway accident.. Through documents found on him, he is identified as Valentine Hooper. Hooper, alias Hitchins alias W.H.Berry is nursed back to health at an inn. There he becomes amorously entangled with the inn keeper's daughter. Not only did she largely engineer the liaison but she was also a ward in chancery. So when they try to elope he is charged with contempt of court. In any case how can he be sure he is not already married? So he decides it is time to make good his escape. Perhaps there is some subconscious attraction for not only does he unwittingly go to Portsea, where he used to live, but he stays in the house where his wife keeps lodgers. There, hardly surprisingly, his memory suddenly returns. . The coincidence in this final twist was specially added to give Berry the opportunity of appearing in a whole series of maritime disguises. They included a diver in his bathing costume with his name, fish, in outrageously large letters. The music was by Howard Talbot and Ivor Novello.

Pinero farces adapted as musicals now seemed a good investment. They were better still if the music was by Howard Talbot for his songs cunningly helped conceal the more outrageous impossibilities in the plot. "The Schoolmistress", another of Pinero's farces, was presented in a musical version with the title "My Nieces" at the Queens in 1921.

In October 1920 there followed "The Naughty Princess", a translation of the French "La Reigne s'Amuse" with lyrics by Adrian Ross. The cast also included George Grossmith and Yvonne Arnaud who helped to create a Gallic atmosphere. Amy Augured, Peter Haddon, Elsie Randolph, Sylvia Leslie and Heather Thatcher were also in the cast.

"The Golden Moth" followed in October 1921. It was the name of a low dive in Boulogne. This time Berry appeared as a down-at-heel Marquis. He was a crook and his chief accoutrement was an enormous bag. Whenever he sat down at a table he used his umbrella to sweep everything within reach , irrespective of use or value, into his bag: bottles, full or empty, ash trays, together with any butt ends, even plates complete with half finished suppers, they all disappeared into his insatiable bag.

In the second act a la-di-da girl sat down opposite him. Disdainfully ignoring his attempts at polite conversation, she proceeded to attend to her make-up. Then, quite without reason, she turns on him and pronounces her unflattering opinion of men. He is so incensed that, after rummaging in his bag, he pulled out a bit of mirror, a razor and retaliates by shaving. Ivor Novello was, this time, entirely responsible for the score.

"The Island King" in October 1922 had Berry as Captain Hoppy. He makes a forced landing on a native island and is subsequently elected king. His reign included dispensing justice - in favour of a small consideration. The piece was distinguished by having the chorus dressed in seaweed. Berry was again assisted by Peter Gawthorne who was also responsible for the book

"Head over Heels", a piece by Seymour Hicks, followed in September 1923. It was a promising show. The only cause for its failure seemed to have been the jinx that is claimed to dog all pieces in the theatre which have a circus plot.

JACK BUCHANAN

The third comedian who dominated musical comedy in the immediate post Great War years was Jack Buchanan. He was distantly related to the whisky family but this was no help to him when he made his debut in a low pub theatre in Glasgow. It was a disaster. There was a slight improvement in Edinburgh when he was greeted in stony silence. He taught himself to dance, mainly through watching Eugene Stratton with his soft singing and soft shoe shuffle. He was an understudy to Stanley Lupino in "All the Winners" and was spotted by Phyllis Monkman. She recommended him to Andre Charlot who was producing "Bubbly". Jack Hulbert, his leading man, was due to join the army and the understudy proved to be hopeless. He was still not an obvious star. It was only through the drawn out and thorough training of Charlot that he eventually attained stardom in A to Z in 1921. Then, by 1922 he was producing as well as starring in the first of his musicals "The Battling Butler" at The New Oxford. It was blessed with one of "Pa" Braham's loveliest songs "Dancing Honeymoon".

James Agate defined his productions: "Was there a plot? Not that you minded. Was there music? Not to annoy anybody. Was there a show? Overwhelmingly so".

This was largely because Buchanan had uniquely re-defined musical comedy. His personality was so strong he was able to do without the traditional comedian. Instead of the absurdity of Teddy Payne or W.H.Berry, he was able to substitute himself as a new generation dude. He certainly showed none of the stupidity of the pre Great War model and he never allowed himself to look ridiculous. High spirits, yes, but rather than participate in high jinks he would express a bemused interest in the cavorting of others. Very good looking, slim, elegant and with debonair nonchalance, women found him a heart throb. Men might not have felt so benign towards him except that he seemed completely unconscious of his charm. Similarly he sang with meaning and distinction but within a limited range so that he never seemed to exert himself. He could act love scenes with conviction and had a sure touch with comedy lines. His timing made quite mundane remarks seem witty. "Are you really a princess?" he asked Vera Pearce to which she replied: "Of course. What else could I possibly be?" "Oh", Jack responded, obviously appraising the weighty lady " I don't know. I thought you might be a hammock tester". His nonchalance was perfect. During the run of "Sunny" one of the cast missed his cue. Jack confided to the audience: "You'll realise Sunny's father is off. Now if you just listen we'll hear him" and as he spoke they could hear footsteps tearing down the stairs. He had to make his entrance the other side. So the audience then heard him running round behind the backcloth. When he eventually came on stage obviously out of breath, he was greeted with an enormous roar of laughter which grew even louder when he could not hide his surprise.

He was no less adept at tap dancing. The Times critic, described him dancing in "Fancy Our Meeting" with Elsie Randolph: "we listen to the slow flip-flap-flop of two pairs of shoes caressing the stage in harmony, it seems as though the dancers are diversifying the silence with an exquisite pattern". .

Fortunately the talented Elsie Randolph had no qualms over assuming ridiculous and unflattering disguises. She could do this for she had a gift for burlesque and was a brilliant mimic.

*Jack Buchanan and Elsie Randolph find a topic for serious discussion in
"Stand Up and Sing" in 1931*

She had reached stardom under classic circumstances. During the run of "His Girl", the leading comedienne had fallen ill only two hours before curtain up. Whilst the management were in agitated conference, Elsie Randolph burst into the room and begged to be let play the part. In desperation they agreed. During the performance she never missed a cue or made a false move. She was acclaimed by the audience and never looked back.

Her complete lack of self consciousness caused audiences to love her and give her their complete loyalty. Once when Buchanan abandoned her for the lovely June, the first nighters would have none of it. The unfortunate June was booed and there were continual interruptions from the Galley "Where's Elsie, then?"

"Toni" opened in May 1924 at the Shaftesbury after enjoying considerable success on Broadway. His devotees were all anxious to welcome him home. But he made his first entrance in typical low key. First came 20 chorus boys, crossing dance step in line from the wings and with their backs to the audience. He was 21st in the chain and when they all turned round and was recognised, he received a tumultuous ovation. Also in "Toni" he set the fashion for the double-breasted dinner jacket. Even the nattily dressed Prince of Wales asked who his tailor was. In this he was in the tradition of such "dude" comedians as George Grossmith who started a fashion with turn back cuffs on his coat, Seymour Hicks, who introduced black silk knee breeches for evening wear and Arthur Roberts with his Coddington top hat. The romantic heroes, such as Hayden Coffin, Bertram Wallis, Harry Welchman and Ivor Novello never really exerted the same influence. Partly it was because their appeal was predominantly to women and partly because they were frequently in uniform.

As a producer Buchanan always kept his company in top form. He had a happy way of making monotonous rehearsals seem almost pleasant. "Sunny" was the first in Buchanan's series at the Hippodrome. It opened in October 1926. It was not really in his style. With a book by Otto Harbach and Oscar Hammerstein and with music by Jerome Kern, it belonged more to the musical romance stable. Indeed, this was the team who, a year later, were to produce the revolutionary "Show Boat". It included two hit songs "Who" and the title song "Don't comb your hair, Sunny". It was a lavish production with a scene of a wedding on board a liner. After a few months interval, "That's A Good Girl" followed in June 1928. It set the style for the rest of the shows in Buchanan's series at the Hippodrome. He went to the Riviera and was shadowed by Elsie Randolph as a lady detective "for reasons" as the Times critic remarked that "got further and further from criminality and closer and closer to connubiality." Jack Buchanan danced an eccentric dance and the Tiller Girls danced with their usual precision. At one point the chorus appeared attired in the most unsuitable form of beachwear even for Nice: silk fringed bathing suits and caps with ostrich feathers. Besides the sparsely of clothing there was not much in the way of a story which was fortunate for what there was seemed to need a lot of tedious explanation.

In March, 1931 came "Stand Up and Sing". Besides Jack Buchanan and Elsie Randolph, Anna Neagle appeared for the first time as a principle. She made a success, though it was evident she had some way to go before she would reach stardom. Sylvia Leslie was also in the cast. The best song in the show was called "There's Always Tomorrow"

In February, 1934 came "Mr. Whittington". It was the story of Dick Whittington but without his cat. Mr. Whittington is thinking about the parlous state of his affairs whilst crossing Piccadilly when he is knocked down and suffers concussion. In his unconscious state he imagines himself to be a Holywood film star, a jockey riding the winner at the Derby and the winner of the Lonsdale Belt at the Albert Hall. The show even overflowed into the realms of the cinema to show him stroking his crew to victory in the Varsity boat race. Eventually he reaches the Mansion House. Whereupon he regains consciousness, to find that his affairs have recuperated and that he is nicely rich.

CHAPTER V
INTIMATE SKETCHES

ANDRE CHARLOT

The exponent of intimate revue par excellence was Andre Charlot. Anglo-Russian by birth, he was thoroughly versed in French revue. He was actually working in Paris when, in 1912 Grossmith brought him over for his productions at the Empire.

In creating his own company, Charlot turned his back on the spectacular Empire and Alhambra shows he had been managing for Grossmith. Instead he reverted to the simple Parisian intimate revues. He had a company of eight or ten talented young performers, able to sing, act and who, above all, had personality. For the same reason he preferred small theatres such as the Comedy and Vaudeville. The scenery was at a minimum with many of the sketches played in curtains. One aspect of the French style he did not favour, however, was the compère and commère. Their absence made the whole evening more akin to a charade, though clearly not amateur. Indeed his revues were always in excellent taste and polished to a high degree.

Charlot also had a flair for discovering potential talent and developing his protégés into star quality. He always looked first for personality for he had no difficulty in teaching technique He would be constantly watching them, studying every little movement. With this ability his chorus line at times included Jack Buchanan, Beatrice Lillie and Jessie Matthews. He employed June for 4 pounds a week and he thought Gertrude Lawrence so lazy she was only worth 3.5 pounds. Added to this he would periodically give her the sack. He was unfortunate. After giving considerable time and patience into developing this talent, he regularly had his stars snatched from him by the other great producer of revue C.B.Cochran.

With a cast that was virtually permanent and a staff of authors and composers practically resident, Charlot's revues assumed a dependable standard. They were smart and pointed yet had an ambiguity which reflected the diverse subjects of the sketches. It was a trait he extended even to the titles: "Yes", "Rats", "Tabs", "Just Fancy" and "Buzz Buzz". Because they meant nothing they showed that the main drawing power lay simply with Charlot.

His first independent revue was "Samples". It opened in November, 1915, at the Playhouse with a book by Harry Grattan, who had already proved his ability under Cochran. The music was by Melville Gideon, whom Charlot had met working for Grossmith in "Kill That Fly". It did not attract much attention. But largely due to the highly popular song "A Broken Doll", Charlot felt that with some alterations it would be worth transferring to the Comedy. He brought in Mabel Russel. She had made her name in the delicate sentimental musicals at Dalys but she also had an irrepressible gaiety and a knack for making supposedly surprise items seem as though they really were spontaneous. She fitted easily and happily into the revue company. With this re-vitalisation, "Samples" recovered sufficiently to complete a run of 362 performances.

This gave Charlot sufficient courage to stage "Some More Samples" though Charlot had it shortened to "Some". It was a sly dig at Cochran who, only the year before, had shortened "More Odds and Ends" into "More". It opened at the Vaudeville in June 1916. Harry Grattan was again responsible for the book. It was at this early stage that Charlot's flair for discovering talent first became apparent, for both Beatrice Lillie and Gertrude Lawrence were brought into the team.

Charlot considered Beatrice Lillie very promising but she caused him constant consternation.

She was essentially a tomboy quite unable to resist a dare. She was none the less feminine. When at last Charlot had taught her discipline, she proved inimitable in her gentle derision of the script. She would lead the audience into believing that she was serious. Then with perhaps just a raised eyebrow or twitch of the mouth she would reduce the situation into pure farce. But in "Some" the hit of the show proved to be Rebla, a juggler. He also practised minimum of effort. Indeed he was so languid he barely had the energy to catch the balls at all and only then when it seemed certain he was too late.

The opening sketch of "Some" cleverly prempted the end. From a darkened stage could be heard the calls for taxis given by the audience leaving the theatre. The evening was largely made up of good natured banter covering everything from the telephone exchange to the Royal Academy.

He followed it in 1917 with "Cheep", another dig at Cochran who had just produced 180 pounds. He brought in Lee White who made her entrance by way of a ladder from the stage box. She was wearing what soon became famous as the three halfpenny dress. It was made out of newspaper. - It was, though, soon to cause her considerable concern when she came across others in the cast busy tearing up bits of newspaper. Then there was a bizarre quartet with Guy Le Feuvre as a Bolshevik pianist, Beatrice Lillie as a Victorian drawing room contralto - complete with gown and train - Alfred Austin was a despairing cellist and Hal Bert was violinist, looking like a frustrated Franz Schubert.

Nor was poor Lee White's concerns confined just to her dress. She was soon being made the victim of impromptu pranks played by Bea Lillie, ably backed by her understudy Gertrude Lawrence. For instance, when Lee White was singing "Have you seen the Ducks go by?" the chorus walked behind a wall so that only their duck hats could be seen by the audience. But Gertie later confessed "I couldn't help making my duck frisk and behave as no proper duck would ever do." Worse, she became bolder and would look over the wall and wink at the audience. Then, as they laughed at her she would laugh back at them. Sometimes she would don a straw hat instead of her duck, at others a moustache.

After America had come into the war, Lee, who was herself American, had a patriotic song written by her husband Clay. It immediately provoked all that was mischievous in Bea Lillie. She would take a place behind Lee marching with obvious mock seriousness as a one person chorus. When Gertrude Lawrence joined in Lee White was understandably furious and complained bitterly to Charlot. He gave both girls ten days notice. However, he was so intent on developing the talents of Bea Lillie, he relented. Then, while he thought Gertrude Lawrence was not particularly important, he still felt it would be unjust to sack her alone. So he kept her on too.

Charlot's next production "Tabs", opened in May 1918. He still included references to the war even though it was now in its fourth year. There was a spy drama, produced to conform to the Government's directive that theatre performances should end early. What had originally been a fast moving drama was now rattled through at break neck speed. There was a sketch of a high falutin' lady dispensing hospitality with tea and sandwiches to her butcher and greengrocer in expectation of receiving preference over delicacies in short supply. Her condescension turns to consternation when the butler announces that Lady Marshmallow has unexpectedly called. Worse was to come. My Lady fails to appreciate the situation and rails against the arrogance of these "trades people" only to be utterly dismayed when she discovers the true situation. "A Matter of Time" took to task all those girls who are always late for appointments. It ended with one young man so overcome when a girl meets him on time he then and there proposes only to discover she is in fact half an hour late for a previous rendez vous.

Ronald Jeans was now brought in to assist Harry Grattan. He was embarking on a career in which he wrote nearly forty shows, including straight comedies such as "Young Wives Tale". He owed his success to competence and wit which he could with ease topple over into the ridiculous. In a typical sketch he had the characters named Evelyn, Leslie, Tony and Francis. An apology made to the audience explained there had not been time to check with the author who were men and who women. But Jeans never let a sketch rest just on some such situation. He always backed it with genuinely funny dialogue

He can also be credited with having invented "list" songs; normally attributed to Sylvia, Brown and Henderson in 1928 and most famously to Cole Porter's "You're the Top" in 1934. But back in the Charlot Show of 1926 and just as wittily, Jeans had contributed:

I'm like a house without a roof
When you're away Dear
I'm like a horse without a hoof
When you're away, Dear
I'm like a door without a latch
I'm like a cabbage with no patch,
I'm like an itch without a scratch
When you're away

Charlot changed tack in "Bus Rush", which opened in December, 1918. He imported several already well known names, notably Nelson Keyes, who appeared as a Chinese Scot and a dour American producer of revue. Also, sitting on a windowsill with Margaret Bannerman, he sang "Coupons for Kisses". Margaret Bannerman as Little Miss Sunshine was coupled in another sketch with Gertrude Lawrence as Mr.Rain, twin figures in a Swiss barometer. Deeply in love they were destined never to see one another. Also there was Walter Williams, who stuttered successfully through the song "k-k-k-k Katie".

In "Just Fancy, which followed in March 1920, Margaret Bannerman sang "Three Little Words" and Walter Williams wondered where flies go in the winter. The finale found the company dressed in accordance with the current vogue for child geniuses. They formed a row of little horrors, sitting along the footlights, reciting their nauseating compositions.

In "Jumble Sale", which opened the following December, Charlot brought Binnie Hale into the company. She proceeded to burlesque Evelyn Laye, Phyllis Monkman and almost half the cast in the musical "Irene". Phyllis Titmus, silhouetted against a white sheet, sang "When the Shadows Flicker" music by Philip Braham.

"Puss Puss" which followed in May 1921, was not one of Charlot's best. It was weak on wit, though that does not mean it was without humour. On the contrary, there was Bert Coot, who had taken over from Walter Williams. He would subtly encourage the audience to join in his songs while all the time pretending to be annoyed at their intrusion. Horace Brown composed verses on words supplied by the audience and made it all look easy.

For a while it seemed that Charlot might be losing his touch. Despite having music by Philip Braham, neither "Pot Luck" nor its successor "Now and Then" was particularly notable.

However, August, 1922 showed he was back on form with the opening of "Snap" An ingenious effect had six girls dressed in black except for whitened faces, white gloves and silver topped canes. Another six were apparently dancing on their shoulders. They were made largely invisible through being in front of a black curtain with the top set on a black shelf. In "Pleasing Everybody", a producer was busy "the morning after" incorporating all the improvements suggested by the critics to the utter despair of the author.

In " Rats", which Charlot staged in February, 1923, Ronald Jeans produced a particularly ingenious batch of sketches. " Incredible Happenings" had a waiter refusing all suggestions of a tip, protesting he had given terrible service. Then there was a family warmly welcoming an income tax inspector. "Pulse of Passion" illustrated the impressions of a man becoming increasingly drunk. First he sees the other characters in duplicate. But they keep increasing and he finally becomes almost hysterical on the entrance of five trim parlour maids. Another sketch showed the different ways of settling disputes. In the West it is by using fisticuffs. Two Chinese, all smiles and politeness, invite one another into the world beyond and in Wally Wally land it is all savage cries and spear thrusts.

Impersonations in this revue came ever nearer home. First Binnie Hale did an impersonation of her father while Alfred Lester had the audacity to burlesque Gwen Farrer, who was appearing in the same show. Gertrude Lawrence in full Ku Klux Klan rig, somehow managed to exude seductiveness while singing about the pleasures of lynching.

"Yes", the last revue Charlot staged at the Vaudeville, opened in September 1923. A young man is anxious to impress his future in-law. He hires an impersonator so that he can claim intimate acquaintance with famous people. However it all comes to grief when he expects Ramsay MacDonald but through a misunderstanding in bursts Flora MacDonald.

"Puppets" opened in January 1924 with Binnie Hale, Frank Lawton and Stanley Lupino. But its great attraction was the songs by Ivor Novello, including "Raggedy Doll", "Italian love" and "What do You Mean?"

Two months before he had staged "Some", Charlot had already started presenting revue at the Comedy. The first was "This and That" with Harry Grattan largely responsible for the book. James W.Tate, who previously had only supplied interpolations, now wrote the entire score. Taking his cue from Jerome Kern, he appeared on stage to play the accompaniment to his songs sung by his wife, Clarice Mayne.

"See Saw" opened in December 1916 and though Charlot called it a musical show it was, in fact, revue. The only really memorable incident was Phyllis Monkman as a Babylon slave who's seductive dancing aroused the interest of Mark Anthony, much to the ill concealed jealousy of Cleopatra. Philip Braham was responsible for the scores as well as working on the Vaudeville revues.

The several faces of Binnie Hale in "Jumble Sale" in 1920. Left, as Phyllis Monkman and, right, as her father Robert playing a male milliner.

In May, 1917, Charlot followed with "Bubbly". The opening sketch had a musical score on the backcloth. Every few moments a face burst through the centre of a note. They belonged to Jack Hulbert, Phyllis Monkman, Whinnie Melville and Jack Buchanan, just starting with Charlot at a salary of 5 pounds.

Current West End shows that came in for comment in "Bubbly" included a highly intense production of "A Woman of Importance" in which a headstrong youth, encouraged by his fond, forgiving mother, falls in love with a lady with a past. And all the while there is a tiresome sage insistently dispensing good advice. "A tooth for a Tooth" was a grand guingol play dreamt by a lady under gas at the dentist

"Tails Up", in June 1918, opened with Jack Buchanan, Phyllis Monkman and the rest of the Comedy company following the debutant vogue for dropping into a cabman's shelter for a meal. The shelter was then used as a sort of scenic compère and commère. It kept on reappearing at the start of each sketch so that it soon became a bore. The individual sketches, however, carried the inimitable hand of Ronald Jeans. There was a forces concert party with the sergeant major as producer, aspiring to a production of Macbeth. The military became the target again as a civilian wanders the War Office corridors hoping to see a general. He grows older and older as he is moved from waiting room to waiting room. When he does eventually reach the inner sanctum it is only to be told his papers are out of date.

In August 1919 Charlot took over the Prince of Wales Theatre. His first production had Ronald Jeans providing numerous " dips" into "Bran Pie". One of the most telling had Jack Buchanan as an aristocratic private under the orders of a plebeian officer.

Continuing to seek an alternative to the compère and commère, Charlot had the much happier idea of using the alphabet in "A to Z" which opened in October 1921. His persistence was rewarded for it was, in fact, one of the most memorable of all his shows. It marked the debut of his long time protégé Gertrude Lawrence in a leading role. She had developed a nervous energy which found a response particularly among the ex servicemen in the audience. She also had an ability vital in revue for learning her lines quickly so that she could incorporate verses of a song written only minutes before curtain up. In "The Oldest Flame", Enid Stamp Taylor reviewed all the famous lovers in literature. "Green Eyed Monster" told a story of jealousy and murder. It had been so badly received by the critics it was thought it might be improved if played backwards. This applied not only to the dialogue but the action as well. Gertrude Lawrence sang "Limehouse Blues" and later appeared alongside Beatrice Lillie in a skit on "Fallen Angels". They were in prams, wearing knitted baby hats and getting tipsy on baby bottles filled with gin. Jack Buchanan alone and in white tie and tails nonchalantly sang his way through "And Her Mother Came Too", though in the programme it was "Too much Mother". Holding a silver knobbed cane in front of him he did not move as he nonchalantly sang it very quietly until the very last line when he gave a little breathly giggle and went into a soft shoe shuffle". The final sketch was a skit on the Russian ballet with Beatrice Lillie as Madame Wanda Allover. She was supported by Mesdames Hangover, Halfseesova, Riteover, Cumova, Pullova, Shotova, Leanova, Beenova, Fallova, Wellova, Tideova and Throwova. The evening was brought to a suitable end with one of Novella's most nostalgic songs, "Night may have its Sadness".

In the mean time Charlot was enjoying an extempore project at the Duke of Yorks. Largely at the behest of his "angel" backer, the young Noël Coward was entrusted with both writing and composing the greater part of "London Calling". .

"The Swiss Brother Whittleboat", introduced brother Sago along with Brother Gob wearing cycling breeches and Miss Hernia in undraped, dyed sacking and festooned with bunches of grapes. Any doubt over the intended implication was decisively dispelled by the immediate and outraged indignation of the Sitwell family. In "Rain before Seven", Coward had Gertrude Lawrence 'phoning all her girl friends giving details of how her ex-husband had thrown himself off a bridge into the Thames. The drama was, however, rather spoilt when the conversation developed into confusion as to which bridge was which and which was the particular bridge in question. In a foretaste of things to come, Coward sang two songs with Gertrude Lawrence, "You were meant for Me" and "Parisian Pierette". In his boundless ambition Coward took a crash course in dancing from Fred Astaire. It was too much. James Agate described him as "self conscious and self assertive". The Sunday Express went further and declared "he cannot compose and should sing only for his friends amusement".

In fact there had been an attempt to spread the risk by incorporating a few sketches by Ronald Jeans. Masie Gay tried to impress her future daughter in law by using modern slang only to become hopelessly confused. Asked about her health she answered "Not so muddy" and then has to explain she was referring to herself only in the winter time. She then went on to appear as a ministering Nurse Doodah, nearly killing her patient with her efficiency and breeziness.

The difference in style between Coward and Jeans was so evident in "London Calling" it ruined any attempt at imposing unity through calling each sketch a telephone call.

Returning to The Prince of Wales in September, 1924, Charlot presented a series of "own name" revues.

"The Charlot Revue, 1924" had above all Beatrice Lillie returning after enjoying a great success in New York. By now she had such a devoted following, Charlot had to arrange two first nights, and as the second house was not due to finish till 3 a.m. a fleet of buses were laid on to take everyone home. Earlier in the evening, a delighted audience had to give Beatrice Lillie protection as she sought refuge from the attentions of an alarmingly over ardent lover. There were sketches by Douglas Furber including "The Influence of the Thesaurus" in which every word was accorded full value through supplementing it with all the alternatives suggested by Roget. The hero asked the girl to be his wife, better half, she, female, missus, bearing squaw, nymph, grissette, mate, whopee, wench or bit of all right.

Peter Haddon and Phyllis Monkman appeared as Mr and Mrs. Noah, singing "The Animals came in two by two". The scene of an Oriental palace was entirely in black and white. The Sultan and his favourites entered, dressed in brilliant rose and gold.

"Charlot's Show of 1926" opened in October 1926. This time the book was entirely by Ronald Jeans, who once more came up with some ingenious ideas, most of them now featuring Jessie Matthews. The opening number was supposed to have been written by the cast themselves. It consequently had outrageously dramatic entrances for each character, not once but several times over.

The revue also included one of Jean's best sketches "Atmospherics". A wireless knob twiddler tunes into three different stations in quick succession. A talk by Dr.Porous Plaster on every day ills and their treatment becomes merged with Major Knapsack describing his adventures in the wilds of Herbacia. Also Mr. Cable is enthusing over Manchester trams so that when a lady in a tram refused a brick layer's offer of his seat he responded by rubbing her chest with camphored oil.

Another Jeans radio sally was "The Price". It was supposed to have been written by an aspiring writer of plays for radio. The butler informs his employer "If you will remain seated as you are, Sir, with the glow of the fire playing on your well cut features, I will see who is at the door". He also suggested three ways to make play going brighter. One was gandguingol enlivened with songs and dances. Another was grand opera but without the music so that the idiotic words and ham acting could be appreciated to the full. The third was a naturalistic ballet with the corps as members of a household joining in the search for father's collar stud.

Another more conventional ballet had Anton Dolin in a skit on the Russian ballet. A rather pathetic note was struck by Herbert Mundin as the last cabby, jeered at by taxi drivers. It was Jack Buchanan's last appearance in a Charlot revue before moving over to a whole series of successful musicals.

And now Charlot's constant stream of productions suddenly stopped as he left the west End for films.

Then, after nearly two years, he returned in August with "Charlot's1928 Revue" at the Vaudeville. However it was in effect an isolated venture. It was chiefly distinguished by Eric Coates' musical version of "The Three Bears". The sketch "Teamwork" had a wife, suspicious after her husband has stayed out all night. She checks by telegraphing six of his men friends. They all reply "Yes, Arthur stayed with me last night".

After a further lengthy interlude, Charlot returned in September 1930 with "Charlot's Masquerade" at the Cambridge. Beatrice Lillie appeared as Clara, Queen of Cowes. She also did a devastating maypole dance while Florence Desmond gave positively the first of what was to prove a world wide excess of impressions of Tallulah Bankhead.

Charlot boosted "Masquerade" into a second edition. It included a vicar who has written his sermon under the influence of American talkies. Also there was a barrister husband cross examining his wife over the breakfast table.

Charlot then went bankrupt, not that such a thing has ever deterred a good impresario. By June, two years later he was back in business with "Faces" at the Comedy. This production had a freshness largely due to the introduction of Arthur Macrae as principal author. He provided Douglas Byng, taking time from the Cochran Pavilion revues, with a song "Trees". He was deploring that he was more sinned against than sinning. He also appeared as a pantomime dame Boadicea in a skit on Cecil B de Mille's "Sign of the Cross", making passes at Ed Chapman's Nero. Francis Day making her first appearance in English revue was Poppia. Edward Chapman was a well inebriated northerner "oop for the coop" Indeed, it was the ninth year he had made the excursion yet he had never actually reached Wembley. Herbert Farejohn contributed "Mad about Noel", the aptly satirical music kindly supplied by Coward himself. Another Farejohn sketch pre-empted the long planned and much discussed Open Air Theatre. However instead of Regent's Park it had been mistakenly set in Hyde Park. Consequently the performance was periodically made inaudible due to taxi doors slamming and riverboats hootimg. Then, as the hero extols the glory of the sunrise, the sky darkens, the cast don mackintoshes and scamper through their lines to finish before the rain. Arthur Macrae also introduced three sportsmen, one a plain cad, another a rotter and the third a bounder, it being finally disclosed that all their sports were indoor ones.

Frederick Ashton arranged the choreography for a striking rumba danced by the chorus silhouetted against a red and yellow striped awning.

Charlot did not do so well with the successor "Hi-diddle-diddle" which opened in October 1934. It did, though, have the benefit of Douglas Byng again. He sang "Miss Otis Regrets" and went on to satirise a can-can dancer of rather advanced age. He ended as an outrageously vivacious Nell Gwyn wheeling a barrow of oranges which bounced strangely like painted tennis balls.

In "Shall We Reverse" which opened in May 1935 Charlot introduced the compère and commère under new guise. A young man is invited to meet his fiancé's grandmother who shows him the family tree. How could he guess that Granny is a witch with intentions? To his astonishment she takes him round the tree. He meets Robert Hale, a 1890's music hall comic. Then on to an excessively formal ancestor living in the deepest bush who yet insists on wearing full evening dress. Indeed formality evidently ran in the family for another forebear was fighting off attacks by the Zulus but unable to communicate with fellow colonialists as they had not been properly introduced.

Then Granny loses control and they flash wildly up and down history. They attend the first night of Aristophanes latest comedy and are invited to the after the show party. Then they meet Sydney Fairbrother trying to sell poison to the Borgias,, rather apprehensively refusing to accept credit. There was even a scene at the opening of the Stonehenge.

By April the same year, Charlot returned to the Vaudeville opening with "Charlot's Chara-banc". "Shake your Spear" was a good deal more amusing than most skits on "Hamlet", particularly as Richard Murdoch appeared as Claude Hulbert playing Polonius, Elsie Randolph was Gwen Farrer as Ophelia, also Jack Clewes as Jack Hulbert as the King. Reginald Smith played Douglas Byng as the Queen. Hamlet, with twinkling toes in contrast to a rigid body topped with elegantly squared shoulders, could only be an impersonation of Jack Buchanan played by Reginald Gardner. Other sketches showed John Tilly as a scout master becoming as tied up as the knots he was trying to demonstrate. Then there were various people dismayed at finding themselves the object of fashion: weary acrobats returning home only to find admirers of Dame Laura Knight's pictures had invaded their parlour; Gipsies cursing Lady Eleanor Smith for all she has written about them in her books. Even the flowers are bemoaning their pansification in the articles by Beverley Nichols.

From this point on, Charlot's productions started deteriorating. Certainly in "Stop, Go", at the Vaudeville in September 1935, there was still a residue of wit. Douglas Byng and Dorothy Ward appeared as two outspoken Ladies from the United States, highly critical of fellow guests at a wedding reception. The humour broadened considerably when it came to Juliet's balcony scene played on the set of Noël Coward's "Private Lives". The action became even more confusing as Romeo started breaking gramophone records over Juliet's head.

But Charlot was losing his touch. It had started with "Stop Go" and now the decline was continuing with "Red, Bright and Blue" at the Vaudeville in 1937. Even the bright part proved to be dull.

There followed his first attempt at spectacular revue in "Dancing City" at the Coliseum. It too failed and Charlot went bankrupt. It was a sad finale for an impresario who had been so successful. He joined Paramount Films as technical adviser but he felt lost in the film world. Eventually he was reduced to taking any walk on parts offered until he died in 1956

CHAPTER VI
STREAMLINED REVUE

C.B.COCHRAN.

It was the circus, visiting the small Sussex village where he was born, that persuaded young Charles B. Cochran that show business was to be his metier. Indeed it was the circus in all its variety and with the continual search for new "turns" that was to lie behind all his theatre work. Early involvements included boxing, roller skating and exhibitions . In the end he settled largely for revue.

While still at school his father's tea and cigar business had failed. Urgently needing to make a living, he tried his hand as an actor in the United States. It was not a success. He did however find success as a promoter of the wrestler Hackenschmidt. Before long he was also acting as agent for Bommbardier Billy Wells, Billy Wilde, Joe Hecket and Georges Carpentier. By this time he was handling big money. So with his love of the Big Top he went on to produce "Fun City" at Olympia and Rodeo at Wembley Stadium.

C.B.Cochran was essentially an entrepreneur. His flair was not so much creative as recognising a growing trend and in hiring potential as well as established artistes. He would scour the world for talent and star them in his revues. It reached the stage when reporters would greet him on landing at Southampton "What have you got new for us, Mr.Cochran". They refused to believe he was serious when on one occasion he replied "A mouth organ player". He was, in fact, referring to Larry Adler at a time when harmonicas were still considered children's toys.

Cochran rarely discovered a British star. Certainly he gave Jessie Matthews her first engagement, but she was still only a child. It was Charlot, though, who groomed her until she was capable of playing the lead. Cochran merely took her over and promoted her into stardom. He could also claim that Anna Neagle, as Marjorie Robertson had been one of his Young Ladies. But it was not till she was playing opposite Jack Buchanan that she first made star billing.

His revues were never condemned for lack of wit. Yet he personally had an almost juvenile sense of humour. Indeed, he often failed to appreciate just how witty were the writers he commissioned, such as Coward, Wimperis and A.P.Herbert His ear for music was equally questionable. During rehearsals for "Words and Music" he decided to drop one of the songs. It was only after furious protests from both Coward and Alice Delysia that he was persuaded to keep it in. It was "Poor Little Rich Girl". He depended on his stage manager, Frank Collins, for all the lighting and special effects.

His strong point as a theatrical impresario lay in winning loyalty among his employees He was loved by even the most temperamental stars. His charm also enabled him to raise the finance to employ talents far beyond the reach of Charlot. It even extended into bankruptcy and a meeting of his creditors ended with them singing "For He's a Jolly Good Fellow" - and - more to the point - a readiness to extend their credit still further.

After his cautious initial productions at the Ambassadors and the failure of 50 pounds due he typically defied the omens and moved not only to the much larger New Oxford but also to the Pavilion which soon became his real spiritual home.

"As You Were" was in itself a far more ambitious revue. Due to the skilful translation by Arthur Wimperis, the book retained all the Gallic wit of "Plus sa Change " by the French humorist "Rip". It satirised war and wartime profiteers. But above all Alice Delysia depicted woman's perpetual infidelity with John Humphries as the perpetual cuckold. To emphasise this, Cochran interpolated Herman Dariewsky,s song "If you Could Care for Me" which was sung periodically throughout the evening.

The first scene was set in 2018 when John Humphries as Sir Bylion Boost becomes so fed up with the philandering's of his wife he takes a pill. But far from giving him solace, he finds himself wandering through history. In his first reincarnation he is Louis XIV romancing with Minon. Sure enough everything is upset with the appearance of Leon Morton as the Compte de Belamy. The action then moves back to ancient Greece. To add to the authenticity, Clifford Morgan appeared as Diogenes, complete with tub. But the story comes back on track as John Humphries finds he has become King Menelaus with Alice Delysia as Helen. Enter Leon Morton as, of course, Paris. Further materialisations included Caesar and Mark Anthony, who is enchanted as Alice Delysia sings about Cleopatra's needle.

Despite all these examples of women's philanderings Sir Billion Boost remains confident he has his wife in check, that is until she volunteers as a nurse on the Somme and seems to be coming unduly concerned over one of her patients - Leon Morton of course. It was at this point she asks the famous question "Are you single, married or in Paris on leave?"

However the atmosphere on the first night was fraught. Uncharacteristically, Cochran's differences with the leading actor, John Humphries, had reached the stage whereby they could only correspond through their solicitors. Matters were not helped by the critics who declared the dresses in the Court of Hungallern to be indecent. They were so insistent the Lord Chamberlain eventually felt he had to demand the clothes be altered. Quite ridiculously they completely overlooked the skin tight black dress Alice Delysia wore as Lucifer. .

With Cochran's revues becoming more spectacular, he gave increasing prominence to his chorus. When passing the programme proofs, an assistant had deleted a phrase imagining that "Cocky was being ridiculous". But "Mr. Cochran's Young Ladies" were soon acquiring a fame of their own; acclaimed as equals to the Ziegfeld girls, of New York. Indeed they followed the original Gaiety Girls by marrying into the peerage. Mimi Crawford became Countess of Suffolk, Tilly Losch Countess of Caernarvon, June became Baroness Inverclyde, Oriel Ross Countess of Poulett and May Etheridge the Duchess of Leinster.

Cochran never missed a trick in promoting his young ladies. When the press asked him to define the difference between his girls and Ziegfeld's, he dreamt up a completely fictitious delineation. It was duly lapped up by the press.

Cochran threw his net still wider for his next revue "London, Paris and New York". It opened in September 1920. Robert Quinault was from the Paris Opera Comique. From New

York came Dorothy Dickson and her dancing partner husband Carl Hyson. London itself was naturally strongly represented with Arthur Roberts, doyen of the musical comedies, singing his old song "In My Handsome". The younger generation was represented by Violet Loraine singing "Whispering". There was Nelson Keyes first as an outsize German bandsman and later as Beau Brummell singing against a Brighton backdrop "The Brummell touch, it means so much". Staying at the seaside, Bunch appeared as Admiral Sir Nash Sark, one of three Whitehall bureaucrats confined at last to their bath chairs. He was joined by Arthur Roberts as Sir Viving Link of the War Office and Alfred Mansfield as Sir Rufus Tape of the Home Office. But there was life in the old boys yet for by the end they had jumped out of their chairs, insisted that their pretty young attendants should take their place and triumphantly wheeled them off.

For good measure, Cochran flung in Spain, represented by Trini, "the most beautiful girl in the world" . Also there was Madam Laura de Santelmo and her company of Spanish dancers in a wonderful Plaza set designed by the leading haute couturier Paul Poiret. They were offset by the Gipsy dancers Maurice and Leonora Hughes. They were only on stage a few minutes but were none the less paid, as Cochran duly trumpeted, the very handsome salary of 150 pounds a week.

"London, Paris and New York" was remarkable for not only was the first half good, as indeed was the case with most of Cochran's revues, but the second half maintained the standard right up to the end. It won unstinting praise from the press.

Cochran staged his next revue at another theatre he had just acquired, The Oxford. It had previously been a music hall. Perhaps this was the reason why Cochran imbued "The League of Notions" with much of the swagger of the old London Pav' and the Tivoli. It opened with a theatre manager lost in a fog. He meets up with some pantomime players who play out some of their ideas to him. Beyond this, however, Cochran abandoned any thought of a linking theme. The whole production simply became caught up in a whirl of spectacle. There were some daring colour schemes, such as the Garden of Dreams with a backdrop of silver - such opulence denoting the presence of John Murray Anderson as producer. Turns ranged from Rita Lee, dancing with a silver balloon which seemed to obey her every whim, while an American appeared in an assortment of masks. Nellie Taylor sang "The Blue Boy", dressed as the Gainsborough model. It was the first Cole Porter song to be heard in London. It was highly topical too, as the picture had only recently been sold in New York for a prodigious sum. "The League" was in no small way aided by the Dolly Sisters. They were a success right from when they made their first appearance clambering out of a giant four poster bed. They reached a peak of sheer enchantment when, with bells round their ankles and tiny cymbals on their fingers, they danced a de Maupassant cameo.

Cochran retained kinship with the music hall in his next revue at the New Oxford, "Mayfare and Montmartre". The cast included Lady Tree, A.W.Baskomb, Joyce Barbour and Alice Delysia, who was sacrificed to the Sun God in a ballet. Ballet was more conventionally depicted in "Door at the Duchess" which featured the Russian ballerina Alice Nikitina. In the finale, the cast appeared one by one down the gangplank of an Atlantic liner, docking at Portsmouth. Alice Delysia was a film star being welcomed by an overawed Mayor. The piece received rave notices in all the local papers during the pre-London tour. But just before the London first night, Cochran introduced a skit on the critics. With all the self conceit of journalists , they forsook their much trumpeted unobjectivity and thoroughly panned the whole evening.

For its successor, Cochran brought his Oxford music hall style to the Pavilion in "Fun of the Fayre". He brought with him his New Oxford author, John Hastings Turner. The opening scene was at St.Bartholomew's Fair set in 1665. Morris Harvey appeared as Samuel Pepys, Irene Brown as Lady Castlemaine, Henry Caine as Charles II and Evelyn Laye as Nell Gwynne. Later Evelyn Laye appeared looking so lovely in a Victorian scene the audience audibly gasped. A subsequent highlight was June and Clifton Webb singing Jerome Kern's song "Who's Baby are You?" Not so successful, though, were the Fratellini. The darling of Paris, their clowning was too crude and on the first night they were hissed off the stage. Cochran had to bring back the Dolly Sisters as an emergency replacement.

In "Dover Street to Dixie", Cochran split the evening as precisely as the title. The first part was British. In "The Dancing Scene", the curtain revealed a charming backcloth, designed by L Walter Murray,. On the right was a dancing master complete with fiddle and on the other side full skirted ballet dancers. Then, surprisingly, the whole tableau came to life.

Cochran allocated the second half entirely to the Salvini Company of America. The cast was entirely black and were led by Florence Mills, who made an immediate impact with her dreamy rendering of "The Sleepy Hills of Tennessee".

For some time now Cochran had felt his revues were too slow. He gave his feelings full reign in his next Pavilion revue "On With The Dance", which opened in April 1925. Both "London, Paris and New York" and "The Fun of the Fayre" had no more than eight or ten sketches. In "Dover Street to Dixie" he more than doubled this. The first half alone had twelve numbers. With "On With The Dance", he doubled this again with 25 in the first half and as many in the second. This was never equalled until Benny Hill's sketches on television.

With such quantity and variation there inevitably arose the problem of the running order. In his introduction to Mander and Mitchenson's photo album "Revue" Coward wrote of how he had learnt the art of this endlessly fascinating and always essential aspect of revue from Charlot: "He would have the names of all the numbers in the revue printed on separate cards, place them on his desk and then, as though playing patience, juggle with them and go on moving them about, shifting them again and again until he was satisfied that they were in the right running order. The finale of the first half would already have been agreed upon but all the numbers leading up to it had to build, and build to the number before the finale and that number, whatever it was, had to be sure-fire. The second number in the second half was, still is, and always will be, terribly important. It has to be so strong, or so funny, or so spectacular or whatever, that the audience, including by then the stragglers from the bar, will settle back comfortably in their seats, happy in the knowledge that the second half is going to be even more brilliant than the first.

"All this can still be done with the cards fairly amicably. Then the fun begins. ' You can't possibly change the set from So And So straight into So And So'. 'Gertie couldn't possibly make the change from tweeds at the end of the sketch into deep evening dress for the beginning of her big number" and so on and so on; more juggling of the cards until all is set and all will run smoothly."

Cochran was able to do this in "On With The Dance" largely through the dexterity of Noël Coward. The sketches had a wide range. There were Ernest Thesiger and Douglas Byng, two lady lodgers in a Bloomsbury boarding house trying to retain their superiority while undressing for the night. The Venetian blind falls down. "Please, please allow me. I'm used to Venetian blinds; we had them in our house at Boulogne when I was a girl".

At the other extreme there was Hermione Baddeley leading a chorus singing "Poor Little Rich Girl" The lyric was a brilliant example of Coward's style of dispensing arch philosophy through leaving clichés hanging meaningless in the air: "Cocktails and laughter, but what comes after, nobody knows.." and "Poor little rich girl, Don't drop a stitch too soon". As purveyor of his own songs, Coward, speeding along the lines with his clipped consonants, considerably assisted this deception.

Coward was one of those stars who are essentially themselves and any attempt to assume another personality is a forlorn hope. It was not an altogether happy situation. He set out to be smart and sophisticated, yet "He never seemed quite able to submerge his lower middle class upbringing beneath his idea of what constitutes a man about town".

Ostensibly the score should have been entirely by "Pa" Braham. But Coward had been stung when Cochran told him his music was not good enough. So he wrote almost every sketch so that it led naturally into a song. At the same time he made his lyrics so off beat the wretched Braham could make neither head nor tail of them. One person alone was capable of setting them to music, Noël Coward.

Even so Coward's contributions were mostly interludes in what was essentially a dance show. There was classical dancing and modern, acrobatic dancing and even contortions. One followed another with breathtaking speed. Key to the whole was Leonide Massine. His pronounced sense of rhythm and clear cut mime was exactly right for producing steps suited for the non balletomane. At the same time they tended to be bizarre rather than charming.

"Crescendo" was in accordance with "Poor Little Rich Girl" in portraying the restless younger generation. It started in a sylvan glade in shades of green and brown and lit in blue. The tempo of the music gradually increases and suddenly the glade is transformed into the flaring contrast of a cubist cafe vivid with jagged black and white lines and extreme angles. Against this setting ,the tempo increased still more until the dances culminated entirely in eccentric body movement.

Another set was a softened version of Hogarth's Theatrical Wild Life, one in his series on "The Rake's Progress". It was set to music by Roger Quilter. It showed the sort of barn the early players would use as a dressing room. It was in sunshine yellow and ochre, the back wall filled with a giant mirror hanging aslant. In front of it were tables with candlesticks holding unsnuffed candles with exaggerated flames. Then the grotesques entered, their bizarre effect heightened through being dressed in contrasting blue.

Another scene derived from a classic painting was the old Moulin Rouge in which Doris Zinkeisen brought Toulouse Lautrec's drawings to life.

The second edition "Still Dancing" was far more relaxed. "The Rake's Progress" was retained, as was a graceful "Hungarian Wedding" which had the brilliant, traditional dresses flooded with orange light. "Crescendo", though, was replaced by the altogether more restful "Pompei a la Massine", inspired by Etruscan frescoes daringly interpreted by Doris Zinkeisen

Cochran had had a momentary disagreement with Coward and replaced him with Arthur Wimperis and Ronald Jeans. A newcomer Vivian Ellis provided the music.

In its successor, Cochran took a leaf out of Charlot's book and christened his 1926 revue personally. He kept the emphasis on dancing which was again excellently expounded by Massine. Typical was a simple mime ballet called "The Tub". Petronella greets her lover but they are alarmed by a knock on the door. It is her husband so Petronella tells her lover to hide in a large tub. But her husband has returned with someone who might want to buy the tub. With great presence of mind, Petronella tells him she has only just sold it herself and the purchaser is actually in it at this moment making sure it is sound. Gianello then crawls out and says he will definitely buy it if the husband takes it home for him. The husband agrees and carries it away leaving his wife alone with her lover.

Another of Massine's ballets was "Gigue" based on themes by Bach. Handle was also recruited as accompaniment to "Three Little Birds" when the beautiful Spinelli had layers of dresses stripped off by jealous little birds.

Non dancers in the company included Hermione Baddeley and Douglas Byng.

Now that Cochrans's confidence in Dixie had been confirmed, he staged "Blackbirds". It was largely the fruits of Lew Leslie's scouring the United States for black talent. Here and there he had found some brilliant artistes, particularly in church benefit performances. The star was again Florence Mills. One of her more successful songs was "Shuffling Along", which ended with a dance with Johnny Nit. There was the more durable "I'm Just Wild about Harry". But her undoubted success was "I'm A Little Blackbird looking for a Bluebird" which perfectly set off her exquisite trills. Johnny Huggins sang an inaudible "Silence and More Silence" culminating with a dance in enormous boots and with an invisible partner. There was an almost equally remarkable dance given by The Four Pullman Porters and The Three Eddies

It introduced fresh qualities into West End show business so that Cochran wrote "Negroes have the grace of born actors, the only danger being their tendency to play white. Coupled with this is utter unselfconsciousness and sincerity together with the most obvious enjoyment in pleasing the audience."

"Blackbirds" had little humour, the sets were not particularly good nor was the score particularly melodious. But it had pure cottenfield syncopation devoid of all the adulterations and finking' detail beloved by the popular bands of the day. But above all it was the drive and tempo which utterly overwhelmed any thought of criticism. The Plantation Orchestra on its own carried the hard headed first night audience into uninhibited cheering.

There was another illustration of the heights Cochran had reached with the opening of his next revue "One Damn Thing After Another". The queue for gallery seats started forming at eight o'clock the evening before . Soon it had become so long the police had to break it up, not allowing it to reform until 5.0 am.

This innate knack of gauging public taste now warned Cochran against increasing the speed of his productions any further. Instead he increased the emphasis on spectacle. This became clear in "One Dam Thing After Another", which opened in May 1927. Indeed, there was a danger of the spectacle overwhelming the stars. This was to a certain extent counteracted by Ronald Jeans's strong touch in the sketches. In "Lost Souls", the producer had forgotten to tell the cast the set had been redesigned So during the course of a searing triangular drama, the three leads entered through the window, admired the twilight in the medicine cupboard and went to bed in a trunk. In "Lady of the Lake" Jeans supposed the curtain had become stuck and two members of the company obliged by giving the audience a running commentary on the sketch being acted behind it. Jeans's ingenuity apparently knew no bounds and "A One Sided Affair" had the sketch seen as from a seat where only half the stage is visible. Finally he served up a musical version of "The Merchant of Venice", which ended with the plaintiff, defendant and the Dodge of Venice joining together for a little song and dance number.

Cochran remained loyal to much the same cast throughout these revues but now be brought Jessie Matthews in as the star. In signing her up he pretended to be beating her down from the 30 pounds a week she was earning with Charlot. He offered her 20 pounds and she stormed out. Cochran sent his secretary to bring her back. He then told her he really had in mind a sliding scale. 60 pounds a week for the next revue, "One Damn Thing After Another"; 100 pounds a week for the one following then 150 pounds and for the fourth 200 pounds. But her debut was not particularly auspicious. She sang Coward's rather cruel song "Gigolo" The girls in the chorus wore little girl clothes along with Oliver Messel's masks of middle aged matrons. But his judgement proved right for next she appeared with Richard Dolman in front of a giant yew hedge lit by moonlight singing "My Heart Stood Still". It was plugged later in the evening when Edyth Baker played it on her outsize white piano. The song was such a success the Prince of Wales asked the band to play it nine times during the Ascot cabaret ball. Cochran later refused Ziegfeld's offer of 2,000 pounds for the rights. In the end he sold it back to Rodgers and Hart for 1,000 pounds. Another Rodgers and Hart number was "My Lucky Star" sung by Mimi Crawford and Richard Hayden. Also in the revue were Lance Lister, Morris Harvey, Douglas Byng , Sonnie Hale, brother of Binnie. and Max Wall with his eccentric dance which made it seem he was double jointed all over.

After this Cochran brought Coward back for "This Year of Grace" opening in March 1928. It was a brave decision for Coward's last three plays had flopped. Coward felt so contrite he offered to relieve Cochran of the contract. But Cochran felt sure his run of bad luck was over. He told him that, on the contrary, he would be putting his name up in lights.

He was right. Coward's inimitable satirical sketches and front curtain interludes along with his highly individualistic music gave "This Year of Grace" a unity almost unique in revue. Many of the sketches compared the present day with olden times. There was "Ignorance is Bliss" portraying honeymooning couples in 1890, and 1928. In "Teach me to Dance like Grandmamma" the first couples danced the polka; the second the mazurka and finally Marjorie Moss and George Fontana led the chorus in an old fashioned waltz.

In similar vein "Rules of Three" had a simple triangle plot but it was shown as it would have been written by J.M.Barrie, Edgar Wallace and Frederick Lonsdale -with butler added.

Coward also showed a clear understanding of ballet and his spoof Prokofieff was a delight. There was Sonnie Hale as a precociously young man earnestly defining "The Legend of the Lily of the Valley" as definitely early 18th century French, smacking of gently undulating country life and then, again, smacking ever so slightly of the debauched life at court."

Extraneous to Coward and in more classical style there was Tilly Losch, making her London debut. She performed a dance with the hands called "Arabesque". Then she was seen framed in a Gothic arch lit to look like stained glass. It led into her dancing with Laurie Devine to Bach's Air on a G String. For Coward's grotesque song, Laurie Devine and Sonnie Hale wore dead white make up to sing "Dance Little Lady". Again the chorus wore grotesque masks by Oliver Messel. Rather than dance they twitched with mechanical like precision. Sonnie Hale featured again in the wistful song "Mary Make-believe". Then he was perched on a windowsill with Jessie Matthews singing "A Room With A View".

Douglas Byng and Masie Gay appeared in several of those front curtain cameos Coward wrote so well. Masie Gay was trying hard to board a bus in the rush hour. She was entirely on her own yet conveyed perfectly all the pushing and shoving of the queue around her. Whenever she did manage to reach the bus it was only to find it full, a situation leading up to the only word: "Taxi". In another piece a little girl at the seaside told her mummy that she had found a great big whale. But it turned out to be Masie Gay this time as a muscular winner of the cross Channel swimming race. She celebrated her triumph with a mock rendering of "Rule Britannia".

In "Wake Up And Dream", Cochran reverted to spreading the talents among several artists. The score was by Cole Porter and included "Let's Do It", sung by Sonnie Hale and Jessie Matthews and "What is this Thing Called Love? " sung by Tilly Losch and Tom Birkmayer.

The book was by John Hastings Turner. One of his best sketches was "Split Seconds with the Great". Noël Coward was seen talking to John Ruskin, George Bernard Shaw arguing with Samuel Johnson as to who was man and super man, Hannen Swaffer impertinently interviewed Mrs.Siddons and finally Einstein was in grave discourse with Isaac Newton.

The ballets included "Gold Rush, San Francisco, 1849" for which Rex Whistler produced one of the finest sets. A view of the promenade in the Old Empire music hall shifted swiftly to the wings showing an arresting perspective of the stage during a performance of "Copelia".

"Wake Up and Dream" ran for a year to the day.

Again ringing the changes, Cochran aimed to make his "1930 Revue" not so much sophisticated as a return to the intimate. The music this time was by the far more conventionally tuneful Vivian Ellis, the dancing was choreographed by Ralph Reader and Beverley Nichols provided a book which was humorous rather than satirical.

It opened in a Hollywood stately pile with pseudo oak beams a jazz orchestra dressed as hunting servants and vulgarly large brandy glasses. Someone in the stalls protested vehemently that the King's English was being murdered. As the objector walked up the aisle she was recognised as Masie Gay who duly joined the company.

Later on she was to perform another of her famous silent sketches. This time she was a late comer taking her seat in the middle of the row. Just as everybody is standing up, she gets her cloak caught up and takes her time to free it. Half way along, she remembers she has not got a programme, then she drops her money. Finally having reached her seat, she blocks the view while disentangling herself from numerous wraps. As an ultimate gesture, she produces an enormous box of chocolates which she rips open, screwing up each piece of paper individually.

Later she appeared as a housewife cooking to the wireless and becoming increasingly flustered as she tries to keep up with instructions. Unfortunately, in her panic, she fails to realise the broadcaster has moved on to gardening hints. Later her kitchen was commandeered by Jack Powell, a versatile drummer, who drummed on everything from the kitchen table to the bottoms of saucepans. Privately he had also drummed on the Duke of Gloucester's pate.

Beverley Nichols also included period comparisons. This time It was just outside the theatre doors in Piccadilly Circus,. The 1830 episode was seen through the eyes of Oliver Messel and showed the romantic meeting between a highlander and a lovely lady, culminating in their elopement in a balloon. 1900 was depicted by Doris Zinkeisen and included Ada May as Vesta Tilley in guardsman uniform singing a contemporary music hall song.

An Oliver Messel white heaven with much cloud in evidence provided the setting for a further number of satirical encounters. Each arrival at the gate was greeted incredulously "But how did you get here?" Nell Gwynne said it to Lord Byron, the Iron Duke to Lady Hamilton, Nelson to Lola Montez. The exception was, the Empress Josephine who immediately broached Mr.Gladstone as to what he really did say in 1817. Masie Gay appeared, still as the flower girl from the previous Piccadilly scene but now dressed in diaphanous white with a halo she had somehow acquired on the way.

The theme was extended with a sketch of a child of the future looking round Madame Tussauds. After making apt comments about Lady Astor and Tallulah Bankhead she comes to Bernard Shaw. "Is he dead yet" which evokes the answer "Not Pygmalion likely". Fearful the remark might cause offence, Cochran arranged for G.B.S himself to be in the stalls on the first night. Laughing, one suspects, out of concern for his public image rather than at any wit, his reaction successfully disarmed any criticism of bad taste.

"Ballet for Hands" showed girls in a box at a Venetian Theatre, wearing crimson dresses, black masks, white wigs and long white gloves in the traditional carnival style. The arm movements were devised by Balanchine.

Against this pleasant, simple motif, Chochran inserted some disconcerting contrasts. One was Noël Cowards song "Half Caste Woman" and another was an eerie ballet by Lord Berners about a one legged freak from a circus. More conventional was Eric Marshall singing to Aida May the Rodgers and Hart Number "With a Song in my Heart".

Again the revue lasted a year -this time to the month rather than to the day.

"Cochran's 1931 Revue" was a hybrid of sophisticated wit and low comedy. Noël Coward provided the sophistication and two American comedians, Clark and McCullogh the slapstick. The pre-London opening was in Manchester where it ran for only 29 performances. Cochran still believed in his formula and brought it to the Pavilion. There it lasted 27 days. It was a formula conceived through a gap in Cochran's sense of humour. None the less he remained so convinced of its viability he was to try it again seven years later when it met with equal disaster.

It was a sad, even ignominious, end to his reign at the Pavilion. But Cochran was amazingly resilient. Almost as if in defiance he moved to the much larger Adelphi. Here he could fully indulge in his love of spectacle. The new series started in September 1932 with "Words and Music", both by Coward, closely associated with his long term friend designer Gladys Calthrop. Without any other contributors, he in effect presented Cochran with a complete package. Cochran was more than happy and at the time wrote "I think the process of unification the most important element in revue today. It is not enough to pitchfork on to the stage a series of sketches, songs and dances. There must be design and form, balance and rhythm and the best way to achieve these objects is to put all your eggs in one basket or, in other words, bank on one man's inspiration and ability to carry out his ideas. A revue with 20 people working on it cannot achieve its ultimate aim". It was a questionable opinion for several of the critics complained the piece suffered through lack of contrast. The opening number had "The Dancing Boys" dressed in black and white. Not that this suggested monotony for they leapt about on and off the revolving stage. All the time their shadows, cast on a swinging background, grew and shrank in harmony with the music.

A typical Coward sketch satirised the vogue among society ladies for organising charity matinees. Ivy St.Helier was the organiser of the tableau, continually bobbing on and off stage until she became hopelessly lost in the Greek Chorus. Lady Godiver scurried across the stage in absurd modesty; Nell Gwynne spilt her oranges and Salome had to dance among them and in her concern, forgot to collect the platter leaving an embarrassed Romney Brent holding John the Baptist's head. It ended with Ivy St.Helier still further embarrassed by the complete absence of bids as she tries to auction off completely useless objects.

Another typical Coward skit gave the Erik Charell Tyrolisation of "Journey's End". Khaki was replaced with exotic costumes, trench warfare was conducted to the song "Wine Women and Song" and the revolving stage spun continuously amid a shower of balloons and streamers.

"Children of the Ritz", was a weak successor to "Poor Little Rich Girl". The chorus in black velvet and with long black cigarette holders, deplored the effect of the slump since it meant they owed enormous sums to Cartier, Molyneux and Arden. Romney Brent really came into his own with the song "Mad Dogs and Englishmen" and Rita Lyle led a chorus of boys in white ties and tails singing "It's The Younger Generation knock knocking at the Door". There was also "Mad About the Boy", a comment on the ridiculous fan mania over film stars. The fans ranged from a love sick school girl to a street walker. Each, spotlighted on different parts of the stage, took over sections of the song without ever disrupting the flow of melody.

Next Cochran moved over to the Palace where "Streamline" showed a return to his more customary style. It opened in September 1934. Its success had been already assured even while it was playing in Manchester. The libraries had put through a sensational deal.

"Perseverance" was a skit on Gilbert & Sullivan's "Patience". A.P. Herbert admirably caught Gilbert's knack of being pseudo portentous with sentences of two words such as "extravagant predicament" while Vivian Ellis exactly hit off Sullivan's way of " leading up to an air only to produce just the air that is expected". In fact, the skit was almost too close to the original so that it produced appreciative chuckles rather than outright laughs

In "Evolution", A.P.Herbert commented on the chorus. First they appeared demure in long dresses going off to post performance assignations in private rooms in Romanos. It ended with the modern girl, in briefest apparel leaving the theatre to bike home to Tooting and a cup of chocolate with mother.

Another sketch showed "Newspaper readers at home", dutifully reacting in the ways anticipated by the media: "The nation was horrified to hear" etc. When the postman brings the "special offer" book, their comments are correctly ecstatic "Isn't it handsomely bound?" and "What wonderfully clear type".

The French clown, Sherlot mimed a goalkeeper making several spectacular saves followed by utter dejection on letting the ball through. He played against a backcloth by the cartoonist Tom Webster showing the crowd with a drawing of 6,000 faces.

Romance and whimsy were served by Tilly Losch in a crinoline, persuading a postman to return a letter she had impulsively written to her lover. Later she was the Duchess of Richmond dancing on the eve of Waterloo in a gorgeous setting by Rex Whistler. She was followed by Jack Holland and June Hart in a ballroom dance. On the first night the audience applauded them for five minutes before it realised Cochran was resolute in his ruling against encores. In "Nowhere to Go", Esmond Knight and Betty Hare were moved on from park bench to park bench by an unsympathetic policeman. Norah Howard, backed by a chorus of nannies wheeling bassinets, sang A.P.Herbert's "Other People's Babies" to Vivian Ellis's catchy air. The evening ended with "Faster and Faster" the embodiment of the title with the chorus dressed as aviators. The tempo increased and increased till the final curtain fell leaving the audience almost as exhausted as the chorus.

With "Follow the Sun", Cochran returned in February 1936 to the Adelphi. Dismissing all thoughts of intimate revue, Cochran primed his publicists to feed the press with a mass of breath taking statistics. There were 1,200 costumes, and most of the dresses required three petticoats. During the evening, each young lady wore 200 yards of material and 60 yards of frilling.

With so much capital tied up, the death of George V just before the opening was a serious set back. But even with the unexpected extension, the dress rehearsal was formidable, even by Cochran standards. It lasted 45 hours, leaving the company only just enough to get into their costumes before curtain up.

"Follow the Sun" showed the degree to which Cochran could count on the sophistication of his audiences, from stalls to gallery. In The Three Kings" Irene Eisinger in a lose blue costume reminiscent of the Madonna, sang a poem by Heine set to music by Ruch in front of a set like a German baroque altar piece.

She appeared, too, as Mozart singing "La Finite Sempliee" at the court of the Princess of Orange. Another of her songs, "How high can a Bird Fly?", admirably showed off her high soprano voice combined with her almost birdlike delicacy of movement. In "Love is a Dancing Thing" she was accompanied by muted instruments against a backdrop of silver blue drapes.

Another memorable singer was Clare Luce. In "Dangerous You" she was spotlighted on an otherwise darkened stage and ended by descending out of sight beneath the stage. It was such a hit that on the first night Cochran had to break his rule and let her take an encore before the audience would allow the show to go on. Clare Luce also appeared as "The Lady With the Tap", a spy dressed in severe black, she made a striking contrast to the Cochran Young Ladies in fine military uniforms. She mesmerises them with her tap dancing until, caught helpless in her rhythm she is able to steal the secret plans. There was Ciro Rimac and his band of Cuban singers. They played their hot, loud, exotic rhythms and dances with exhausting energy against a tropical setting of violent reds, greens and purples. Then the stage revolved to show Lance Fairfax singing "Nicotina" against a background of luscious tropical green flora.

A ballet "The First Shoot" was a remarkable combination of talents. The choreography was by Frederick Ashton, decor by Cecil Beaton, music by William Walton and story by Osbert Sitwell. Outlining the piece in a programme note, Sitwell wrote "The action takes place in a woodland glade, during a fashionable Edwardian shooting party, the first to be given by Lord de Fontenoy since his marriage to the lively Connie Winsome, late of musical comedy. After an opening dance of pheasants, Lady de Fontenoy enters soon followed by her admirer Lord Charles Canterbury, who performs a dance for her pleasure. But they are interrupted by the rest of the party, who march round firing in the air and then off to luncheon. Lord Charles lingers, fires at another bird and accidentally wounds Lady de Fontnoy. Dragging herself onto the stage, she dies in his arms, to the intense interest of the other guests""

The finale first showed the exterior of an ale house in 1845 with all the cast dressed in wayfarers costume. Then followed modern Hyde Park with a full sized merry go round complete with prancing horses. They revolve as snow starts to fall. It grows thicker and thicker until the curtain falls on the stage empty except for the whirling snow.

Cochran's "Coronation Revue" opened in February 1937 and the title was soon changed to "Home and Beauty". He reverted to linking all the scenes to a theme. In this case it was a week-end house party at Mulberry Moat. With the exception of the impersonators Binnie Hale and Nelson Keyes, all the guests retained the same characters throughout the week-end. It opened on Friday afternoon with the entire household assembled to welcome the guests. The hall had a steeply curving white staircase on one side and enormous red Figaro windows on the other. Some of the sets had plasterwork taken from actual carvings of Grinling Gibbons. Some of the chairs were genuine Sheridan and the clothes were designed by the Queen's dressmaker, Norman Hartnell.

In "Dressing for Dinner", eight Cochran young Ladies were discovered in front of eight little dressing tables with oval mirrors. Each is wearing peach coloured cammy knickers. Then they give place to eight men who adjust their ties. Finally the girls reappear in green dresses with purple overnet, ready to go down for dinner.

But for some of the guests preparations are not going quite so smoothly. Nelson Keyes is Sir Lazarus Moon, the richest man on earth, with 40 pairs of trousers and only one pair of braces - and those he has mislaid. Keyes was seen conducting impressive financial deals over the telephone. But he needs to cross the room and realises he cannot do it whilst holding the telephone, the receiver and his trousers. In a few gestures he reduced a mighty tycoon into the most vulnerable of men.

At the same time Binnie Hale, from Covent Garden, via Hollywood, is singing gently to herself in her bath. However the neighbouring bathroom is occupied by Gitta Alpar, a jealous primadonna from Buta Pesth. Before long their simple ditties have developed into full blown rival arias of Verdi and Puccini.

At dinner the cast drank the royal toast and, on the opening night just before the Coronation, the entire audience stood up too.

After dinner, in the music room, the guests were entertained with duets by the pianists Rawicz and Landauer. Later they were joined by Gitta Alpar who sang "Twilight". In the tapestry room, the tapestries came to life to show the story of English coronations down the centuries.

The next morning, Nelson Keyes as MFH leads a mechanised hunt. Binnie Hale appeared as a masseuse working on an old gentleman in a bath robe. During her work she inveigled against men emphasising her points by thumping her patient. Up in the nursery the children are playing at co-respondents and divorcees and down in the kitchen, Binnie Hale and Nelson Keys have come together as tweeny and plumber to sing "A Nice Cup of Tea".

The finale on Sunday evening was in the hall again as the guests depart.

Cochran's next and final revue at the Adelphi was called "Happy Returns". He could hardly have made a more unfortunate choice. Perhaps it was due to his limited sense of humour that he was still determined to mix highly sophisticated and low comedy. He signed up Beatrice Lillie with Bud Flanagan. In one sketch they played Helen and Paris. It was so wildly farcical it almost looked as though the experiment might succeed. But the fault lay deeper. The audience was unable to switch within the time of a blackout from Bud Flanagan's buffoonery to the apparent uncontrolled way Beatrice Lillie's corsage bounced up and down as she sang "Rhythm". As a New York first nighter, her constant chatter completely ruined John Gielgud's "Hamlet" . Finally, perched on a property moon she was swung out over the stalls dispensing far more than the statutory number of garters. Inevitably the moon developed a disconcerting wobble so that she had to abandon her carefree disposition and cling to it for fear of falling off.

With the outbreak of war, Cochran realised that the style of spectacular revue which he had made so particularly his own, was no longer possible. His two wartime revues, the final two he ever produced, were, in fact, a return to the intimate.

"Lights up" which opened at the Savoy in February 1940 had a book mainly by Ronald Jeans and music by Noel Gay. The curtain rose on a blacked out stage with the street walker mistaking a lamp post for a muscular customer. There was a German propagandist reminding the British radio listeners of atrocities committed by the French. at the Battle of Hastings. They were all jokes which would have seemed just as pertinent during the First World War. The revue did not really light up until Evelyn Laye sang "You've Done Something to My Heart". She also outswaggered a swaggering pantomime Prince Charming. But it was at the time of Dunkirk and the Battle of Britain and it barely reaching a hundred performances.

In May, 1942 he presented "The Big Top". With the same theme as had motivated his life in show business, it should have been a triumph. It, too, suffered from incompatibility, this time between the two types of revue Cochran had so successfully produced in the past. It had all the material of an intimate revue but was lost in the tent like vastness of His Majesty's Theatre. Neither Herbert Farjeon's wit nor Beatrice Lillie's minimal gesture could cope with the necessary projection. There were two songs which normally Bea would have made inimitably her own There was a mock pastoral ditty describing the charm of the birds she could watch from her windowsill. But her soliloquy was periodically shattered by the banging of the shutters. Eventually she was provoked into admitting she could not tell the difference between a robin and a blackbird. Even more unaccountably, she failed to hold the audience with "Wind Round my Heart" which soon became one of her most popular songs.

After this Cochran returned to his beloved Adelphi, producing a series of three musicals by A.P.Herbert and Vivian Ellis. One was a triumph and two were failures. Cochran was still optimistic, still planning, when his life was cut short through scalding when his bath tap became stuck.

THE HULBERTS

Jack Hulbert, son of a specialist in speech defects, was studying history and psychology. But rather than writing theses on such erudite subjects he spent much of 1913 writing sketches for "Cheer-oh Cambridge" . He played the lead as well. And that is when he was talent spotted by Robert Courtneidge, producer of the enormously successful musical "The Arcadians". He signed him up for his new musical "The Pearl Girl".

It was not long before even Courtneidge, renowned throughout the theatre as a slave driver, was praising the way the young man rehearsed and polished his performance. Indeed, Courtneidge listed him among the four hardest working actors he had ever known.

Playing opposite Jack Hulbert in "The Pearl Girl" was Courtneidge's daughter, Cicely. Papa had been ruthless in preparing her for the stage since the age of six. She had learnt elocution, to play the piano, to sing and dance. But while she could do them all competently, she performed without any noticeable flair. At fifteen, her father told her bluntly she was not good enough even in the chorus. As he had hoped, it shocked her into appreciating the difference between cursory and fanatical application. Within months she had so improved he felt he could justifiably put her into the show.

It was through this determination and hard work that the two youngsters found mutual respect. From there it led to love and eventually marriage.

While Cicely was not stout, she certainly had presence and it was only to be expected that throughout their career on stage she was always to the fore. Jack was the power behind her but on stage she simply assumed the leadership. She had an excellent sense of timing and mimicry. When inspecting school girls lined up as a guard of honour, her about turn was a brilliant distillation of every sergeant major.

Initially, though, their professional partnership was short lived. Robert Courtneidge went broke. After further bitter financial experiences, Cicely achieved a steady living on the music halls. Jack Hulbert joined the army and on his demobilisation found a place in the new revues of Andre Charlot.

In 1921, the two came together again in "Ring Up" at the Royalty. It was a disaster. So Jack returned to Charlot and appeared in such revues as "Bran Pie" and "Pot Luck". In the mean time, Cicely abandoned the halls for domesticity.

Their next opportunity to appear together was in the Little Theatre revues. The first "Little Revue Starts at Nine" opened in October 1923. Harold Simpson, Reginald Arkell and Douglas Furber wrote the sketches and lyrics while Herman Fink provided the music. The Hulberts had two numbers together: "Top hat and Tails" and "Two Freshers". They also had a sketch illustrating the different approach to card playing in Mitcham and Mexico. It was the first time Jack had written for the professional stage.

A second edition "Starting at Nine" opened in March 1924. In one of the sketches, the lights suddenly failed and once they had been restored it was discovered that a valuable picture had been stolen. The distraught host explained to his horrified guests that the painting was not really valuable - indeed the frame cost more. Then it is suggested the lights should be turned off again to give the thief the opportunity to make amends. When switched back on, the painting had indeed been replaced. Now it was the frame that was missing.

Jack then adopted the Little Revue formula for "By The Way" and built it around the two of them. He also proved highly adept at polishing the chorus to a precision outstanding even in spectacular revue. Although Harold Simpson and Ronald Jeans stayed on from the Little Revues, Jack wrote a number of the sketches himself and much of the music was by Vivian Ellis.

Ronald Jeans had come to the fore in Charlot's two immediate post war revues. He had an almost inexhaustible fund of quirky ideas. In this case he had the audience privy to a radio studio during a highly dramatic play. "Unhand me villain", shrieks the heroine as she calmly polishes her nails. All the while Jack Hulbert, as effects man, astonished the audience by producing the most unexpected sounds from the most improbable gadgets. As the hero finally swears undying love, he takes the other girl out to supper. The devastatingly beautiful heroine slaps a highly unprepossessing hat on her head saying: "Thanks God that's all over".

The subtlety of the Hulbert touch was seen as a master keeping naughty boy Cicely back in classroom after hours . However the school cricket match is being played just outside. Sounds from without, indicating success or failure, cause surreptitious glances from both master and pupil, making it clear the punishment was just as agonising for both.

Hulbert was always generous in playing second to Cicely. This was clear when Cicely appeared as an elderly widow pretending a coy like innocence on her second honeymoon.

Having taken the initial step into management, the Hulberts had, by 1927, found the confidence to move to the much larger Adelphi theatre. There they embarked on spectacular revues..

In taking this decision they were largely in step with C.B.Cochran. Indeed throughout the theatre there was growing alarm over the threat of the cinema now that it had developed a voice. Alfred Butt was determined to beat the films at their own game. In 1925 he staged "Rose Marie" with a series of fabulous sets and a sensational chorus. The panic was to last until 1934 when Erik Charell staged his third and greatest fling with the revolving stage at the Coliseum. "The Golden Toy" proved an expensive flop. On taking stock, it was clear the West End theatre was completely unaffected by the talkies

The cinema did, however, educate audiences to accept swift cutting. Keeping in step, the hour long scenes in the theatre or ten minute turns in variety became much shorter. Similarly sketches in early revue had often lasted twenty minutes. Now they were a mere three or four minutes.

The first spectacular revue staged by the Hulberts was "Clowns In Clover" which opened in December, 1927. The chorus was accordingly enlarged and June and the much admired Duncan Sisters joined the cast. Vivian Ellis was again the composer, this time aided by Noel Gay.

Ronald Jeans was again the author. A typical Jeans sketch, "The Smart Set" occurred because the producer had not allowed sufficient time for the cast to change. Consequently Cicely

Courtneidge appeared as a smart friend of the family, dressed as a cyclist, the father as a boxer, the mother as a hula hula girl, the daughter as a cook and the butler as a seaman.

Another Jeans effort was "Street Professions" when a doctor, adopting a stethoscope as his advertising sign, is offering his services with medicines thrown in, all at bargain prices. There, too, was a clergyman willing to marry or christen at reduced rates.

In "I'll Give you A Ring", a young man makes a blind supper date with a girl. It soon becomes clear she is a telephone operator as she talks relentlessly throughout the meal in professional jargon.

"Clowns in Clover" also contained one of Cicely Courtneidge's most successful sketches. She asks the shop assistant for two double damask dinner napkins. Asked to repeat the order she gets it confused. The assistant tries to help but only becomes more confused. After hilarious tongue twisting attempts she ends by simply asking for twenty four serviettes

In a burlesque of the Folies Bergere , Cicely Courtneidge succeeds in putting her foot through Jack Hulbert's straw hat and in a disastrous finale is carried off by the chorus upside down.

Cicely Courtneidge also sang numerous songs, most notably "There's a trick'n pick'n a chicken".

Strangely much of the impersonations were left to Elsie Janis who duly dispatched Will Rogers, Sophie Tucker, the Two Black Crows and, inevitably Tallulah Bankhead.

A second edition "New Clowns in Clover" was not so successful. Cicely Courtneidge had only one outstanding fresh sketch. The coming of sound had caused consternation among the stars of the silent screen. In "Silence is Golden" a Captain in the Guards is found to have an Irish brogue , the sexy vamp speaks in guttered English the formidable chief of the Gipsy has a pansy lisp and the star herself a cleft palate. .

Continuing at the Adelphi, "The House that Jack Built" opened in November 1929. The music was again by Vivian Ellis, this time aided by Ivor Novello. Best of the Ronald Jeans sketches illustrated two versions of a dinner party conversation. First the guests conformed to conventional conversation. Then they covered the same topics but giving voice to their thoughts.

Cicely Courtneidge appeared in her customary numerous guises, including a crushing country post mistress, a formidable dowager and a fairy queen emerging from her blasted oak and completely dominating the shrinking demon king. "The House that Jack Built" had one particularly successful sketch which , like the double damask dinner napkin sketch was made into a record. By some accident, laughing gas escapes in a solicitor's office during the reading of a will. As the conventional reading proceeds, Cicely Courtneidge leads the relatives of the deceased first in overdone reverence, then smirking slightly, then giggling, laughing and finally the entire family and the solicitor are in hysterics -

She also appeared with Jack Hulbert as a middle aged lady meeting a former lover. She keeps cutting short his romantic reminiscence with down to earth advice over cooking and health hints. The hints are, apparently, instantaneous for by the end Jack is holding Cicely by the legs like an ice skater and whirling her round and round.

Jack Hulbert was also active on his own, dancing a political speech. He also modestly admitted he could play the cello - just a bit. He was even prepared to play requests from the audience. However his interpretation of the requests always seemed to dissolve into "You're the Cream in my Coffee".

Then disaster struck the Hulberts. Cicely could not understand why her cheques kept bouncing. It then emerged their business manager had lost all their savings. on the Stock

Exchange. They found that, even with their prodigious energy and capacity for hard work, they would in practice earn more if they split up. So Jack began starring in other people's musicals. Cicely joined Nelson Keyes in "Folly to be Wise" opening at the Piccadilly in January 1931.

Though not appearing in the revue Jack, as producer, ensured continuity of style. Additionally Vivian Ellis continued to supply the music and Ronald Jeans the book.

It started with the whole cast emerging from an enormous pierot hat. In another spectacular scene the set was mounted on one treadmill and the chorus on another, revolving at different speeds until the music brought each into the correct combination .

Among the Jeans inspirations Cicely Courtneidge was an elderly tourist in a Paris restaurant, happily unaware that it was patronised by the underworld. She gaily prattles on about the vicar, quite unaware the person at the next table has just been stabbed. She also appeared as a nervous member of an acrobatic team going to great lengths to avoid her turn to be thrown. Then she was a rather pathetic old lady, being subjected to a ruthless salesman anxious to convert her family home into a cinema. Only after the salesman has left, convinced he has driven a hard bargain does it emerge that it is not really the family home. On the contrary it is uncomfortable, damp and dark and the old lady is heartily glad to be rid of it. And finally Cicely joined forces with Nelson Keyes to sing Noel Gay's highly successful satire on the pomp, the uniforms, the scarlet, the gold and the all the King's horses brought out just to "put a little pep into the Lord Mayor's Show".

Nelson Keyes' skill at character drawing was shown to the full through impersonating various types of employee being sacked by several sorts of bosses.

The chorus of Tiller Girls danced with infectious rhythm and precision gestures. Later they were seen having supper, each at her own little table and later getting into a little white wooden bed - but only after having placed their shoes neatly at the foot.

The second edition of "Folly to be Wiser" opened in the September. Additional numbers included a "chocolate box" interpretation of "Milking Time in Switzerland". Then Cicely appeared as a fancy dress Lucretia Borgia getting gently tipsy on port. Together with Nelson Keyes, she sang a sequel "The Kings Navee". It was not so good.

But the Hulberts had discovered they could repay their debts even more quickly through working in films. So it was not until 1938 that they were to be seen together on the West End stage. It was in a series of musical comedies at the Palace starting with "Under Your Hat".

GEORGE BLACK

When George was born, his father was still proprietor of some touring waxworks. The models were happily adapted to appeal to the latest local sensation. Visiting a Welsh town, Little Lord Fontleroy was quickly changed into a recent murder victim Little Willie Llewellyn. As Sir Charles Dilke had a beard, he overnight became the huntsman accused of Willie's murder. It was a world in which young George learnt to gauge and respect the public mood.

George was sent by his father to buy a few films to show in the flea-pit cinema he had recently converted from a church. George returned having spent 3,250 pounds. Not only was it a fortune but he had spent it all on just one film. Fortunately for George it happened to be "Tilly's Punctured Romance", the first and one of the greatest of Charlie Chaplin's comedies.

When his father died, George and his brother Alfred were soon dreaming up sensational marketing techniques for their cinema. They loved doing something different, even outrageous.

When they were showing the film The Flesh and The Devil", they had the cinema floodlit a hell fire red and an embarrassed doorman was dressed as Satan complete with horns.

George's professional axiom was that entertaining the audience begins at the entrance. He observed it through out his career and people queuing for a Palladium show might well find they were being entertained by one or even all of the Crazy Gang.

George took charge of the Palladium in 1928. It was not until seven years later that he steered his productions away from variety until they had, in effect, become revue. Then there came the disturbing discovery that due to contract arrangements he must find places immediately for three of his best double acts or he would loose them to the rival Stoll management. Nor could he split the pairs since each had been together for fifteen years or more. In desperation Black put them altogether into his new Palladium revue. He gave them a month and, in a moment of inspiration, told them they could do whatever they wanted so long as it did not offend the Lord Chamberlain. It was the first time they had all worked together. But it was not that easy. At first Nervo and Knox refused to be on the same bill as Naughton and Gold. But once they had been persuaded, Nervo and Knox insisted Eddy Gray should be brought into the team. But that was not the end to the troubles. After the first few weeks, Black decided to bring in Flanagan and Allen. Flanagan could switch the mood of an audience almost instantly from laughter to sentiment with his Jewish approach to songs. But they were punning enthusiasts and essentially static. They did not seem able to enter the spirit of spontaneity, requiring them not only to run about the stage but among the audience, up the aisles and even popping up in the boxes. It reached the stage when Flanagan and Allen asked to be relieved of their contract. But Black was adamant, even after Caryll and Mundy had felt so strongly they had left. So the penultimate gang comprised Flanagan and Allen, Nervo and Knox, Naughton and Gold and Monsewer Eddy Gray.

They immediately found a common bond not only through their sheer professionalism but through a common passion for practical jokes. They butted in on one another's turns and would even exchange roles The effect even spread to the Palladium clocks which became subject to sudden and unaccountable switches both forward and back.

In fact, of course, chaos only appeared to reign. Such profusion of jokes could only be carried out if backed by relentless rehearsal and perfect timing. It applied not only to the Gang but to a highly trained stage staff. For instance their shows usually had a sequence know as "cross overs". Up to fifty props, ranging from a stuffed horse to a jar of dried peas, would be handed out from the wings on one side, carried across stage with an appropriate witticism, and taken in on the other. A girl wearing a grass skirt might run shrieking across the stage. Close behind her one of the gang would be chasing her with a lawn mower. In another show, the girl would be in armour and the gang member carrying a blow lamp.

It was a technique George Black applied to all his productions, with or without the gang. Rush things on and pull them off before the audience had time to search their memories. With this technique one of his revues might easily require twenty tons of scenery, four tons of props and three tons of costumes.

Much to Black's surprise, The Crazy Month proved such a success it was repeated and inevitably went on to become a revue in its own right.

Officially they claimed the apparent chaos was evolved by allowing "it to mature gently". This in fact meant experimenting and re-writing their ideas. They would even incorporate their private jokes but it made no difference, the audience laughed just the same. They also had mutual respect for one another and if it was felt one of them did not have a sufficiently significant part they would enlarge it in some other way. The job of co-ordinating the whole was usually left to Jimmy Nervo. He had a sure instinct over how audiences would react.

With this chaos the gang were, in fact, breaking down the formality of revue and substituting the continuity of the musical comedy plot. There were no sketches as such. There was none of the finality of the black out creating a complete division between one sketch and the next. Certainly the curtain fell occasionally but it was merely to allow a change of scene. Even the entertainment would be continued in front of the curtain or, as often as not, in the auditorium or in one of the boxes In this way the Gang was able to create the same cumulative laughter that musical comedy has when the plot ensures ridiculous situations follow close one upon another.

Their first titled season was "Life Begins at Oxford Circus" in 1935. Strangely it was not so much built around the Crazy Gang, as they had now become, as around the band leader, Jack Hylton. Several members of his band had lines while Hylton himself actually appeared in some of the sketches. When he appeared in a scene supposed to be at the stage door the audience accepted him as being part of the off-stage staff and found it all the more hilarious when he was immediately deprived of his trousers.

The penultimate in chaos was a sketch "First Time Here" when supposedly provincial artists were given a chance to show their talents before a West End audience. Going on stage, several were greeted by fond relatives in the stalls. So they, too were invited to come up and have a go. By the end the entire contest was completely out of control.

Frequently there were guest artists, though not all of them could cope with the tempo. One who managed to hold his own was Stanley Holloway. As soon as he was allowed a reasonably quiet moment he told the audience how the lion at Blackpool Circus had sicked up Albert. His father, horrified at the thought of losing the insurance money, quickly sends his son to the tiger cage in the hope they might do better. He also joined the gang as flower girls in Piccadilly Circus. But he could never be sure about his basket. One night it had been lined with lead and on another it had been screwed to the stage and on yet another occasion it was attached to a string and periodically took off into the flies. Another game star was Binnie Hale and although she was also subjected to the treatment, she never failed to give as good as she got. They were just as merciless among themselves. On more than one occasion Môn sewer Eddy Gray's club juggling act would come to immediate disaster because his clubs had been greased. Flanagan and Allen sang their famous down-and-out duet "Underneath the Arches"

In "Roundabout Regent Street", opening in 1935, the Gang really let rip. The show opened with six genuine Herculean acrobats. But even as they formed a stupendous pyramid a little bald man was noticed industriously climbing to the top. Immediately three onlookers sprang forward and in a twinkling he too had lost his trousers. From then on things went from bad to worse. In "The Very Merry Widow" Nervo was an outrageous flaxen wigged, grossly flirtatious widow and Knox a desperate Danillo. Flanagan was Pompus, the State Secretary "who had frequent and hilarious lapses into the mannerisms of Jewry." In this version, the customary climax of the waltz scene ended with playful bitings and rhythmic clawings on an Edwardian settee.

There was a sketch of prehistoric Regent Street. Events included a local Grand National, won by a Brontosaurus. Spectators could buy terrified maidens from a "Stop me, buy one" tricycle. Flanagan as a bookie warned his partner, Allen, against counterfeit stone coins: "There's a lot of cement knocking about". A spectacular scene set in Vauxhall Gardens in 1750 showed ladies, regardless of the anachronism, singing about "Love's a Telegraph". Things rapidly deteriorated, as things had a habit of doing whenever the Gang was about. No matter that they were dressed in elegant silk knee breeches, they proceeded to sing an outrageous song with eight bridesmaids. Then came the quiet, nostalgic moment when Flanagan and Allen sang "They're building flats where the arches used to be".

In 1936 there was "O.K for Sound" The opening sketch showed the shooting of a musical film in the Goldray Studios with the boss Jake Goldmine, admirably played by Joe Hayman furnished with an extravagant nose. Teddy Knox revealed an unexpected ability at impersonations

George Black sometimes gave his spectacular scenes a streak of patriotism which ranged from the extravagant to bordering on the ridiculous. On the evening of the abdication, he had Edward VIII speech broadcast to the audience and instructed the band to follow it with "Land of Hope and Glory" and the National Anthem. There was not a dry eye in the house. With "O.K. for Sound it was the navy that was given the treatment. It started with Drake playing bowls, went on to show Nelson in the Victory and ended with a tribute to the latest pride and joy to Britain's seagoing tradition, the Queen Mary. So for the Gang this was, to a degree ,a comparatively quiet production.

Not so, however for George Black. He had encouraged the gang to extend their performance into the theatre and now they were carrying it into his administration offices. He would arrive for an important business appointment to find the place overrun with Italian child dancers convinced that to be found leaping and jumping was the one requisite for being given a part. Another aspirant, deluded in much the same way, kept passing though crying out in ringing tones "No, no, you don't, Mr. Firkenshaw".

Ian Bevin, in his book on the Palladium, records that George would get his own back. Whenever an offending gag or piece of business cropped up during rehearsal, he would stop them and ask how it had found its way in. The Gang's stock response "It just crept in" to which Black, ever mindful of the Lord Chamberlain, had a stock riposte "Well, let it just creep out."

If there was a particularly outrageous deviation, Black would summon a rehearsal for ten o'clock the following morning. Not only did all the gang live in Brighton but they were late risers. A morning rehearsal was their most dreaded punishment - and Black knew it. He also made sure in a sterner way the gang realised that none of them were essential to the formula. He would sometimes drop one or other from a show.

Roudisim returned in full force in 1937 with "London Calling". First there was Nervo and Knox as guardsmen on sentry duty mounted on stuffed horses and being barracked by the rest of the Gang. But perhaps the highlight was the burlesque of an Elephant and Castle drama with Flanagan as the heaviest of villains, glowering of eye, and playing extravagantly for audience hisses. Gold was a gipsy kidnapping specialist and Naughton as the kidnapped child in yet another of his ghastly flaxen wigs. However the drama somehow ended in complete harmony with the entire gang singing "Heaven will protect the Vicar's Daughter". What from was never specified but the asides gave the audience a good idea.

In October 1939 Black staged "The Little Dog Laughed". It duly incorporated anti Nazi jokes as when five pairs of bloomers were hanging on the line. They were labelled Hitler, Himmler, Goebbels, Ribbentrop and a very large pair for Goering. This gave George Black the idea for the song "We're going to hang out the Washing on the Siegfried Line".

George Black was personally responsible for several other songs that distinguished "The Little Dog Laughed". There was "Franklin D Roosevelt Jones" which Black had heard in the United States and which Flanagan now made into an even bigger success this side of the Atlantic. It was Black, too, who spotted some verse in the Salvation Army's paper "The War Cry", called "You can't Ration Sunshine". He duly purloined it and had it set to music. Then there was Flanagan's number "Any Umbrellas" with the chorus all carrying brollies in various stages of dilapidation. Finally they sang "John Brown's Body" to the words "We pull the damper out, we push the damper in but the smoke goes up the chimney just the same."

Now, well into the war, the Crazy Gang disbanded.

Black introduced Tommy Trinder as leading laughter maker at the Palladium in "Top of the World". The music was by Harry Parr-Davies. For the first night, Black aimed to harness the raucous laughter of servicemen by sending a large batch of first night tickets to the Y.M.C.A There was consternation when they entirely failed to react. This was particularly strange since one of the sketches had Nelly Wallace with Billy Merton in what must have been the most extraordinary Romeo and Juliet balcony scene. Eventually it was discovered the tickets had been distributed in the International YMCA and none of the servicemen could speak English. Despite this, all was set for a long run. But within the first week the Blitz began and a landmine became lodged in the Palladium roof.

By March, 1941 the blitz had subsided a little and Black transferred "Apple Sauce" from the Holborn Empire. Never drawing a distinct line between music hall and revue, "Apple Sauce " was, if anything, tending more to music hall. Max Miller was in a Home Guard squad supposed to be watching for parachutists. He was, however, showing far keener interest in the charms of passing ladies, even though they were obviously spies.

After "Apple Sauce" Tommy Trinder emerged as star again in "Gangway", which opened in the following December. Almost in Crazy Gang style, he kept up a stream of backchat all the time Ben Lyon was patiently trying to explain a rather strange and very involved Chinese drama.

Trinder's humour depended on his calculated egotism - which was enormous. He was the first person to dare remonstrate directly at latecomers: "Get yourself mechanised, Sir". He made a habit during each performance of giving away dozens of photographs of himself. Then, when he felt he had definitely "arrived, he had posters with his picture put up at his own expense all over London with the catch line "If its laughter your after then Trinder's the name".

So successful was his perky type of humour, especially during these war darkened years, George Black kept him on for the next revue "Best Bib and Tucker". It opened in November 1942. Trinder planned a simple front curtain number. He would dress as an over the top Carmen Miranda and sing "No, No, No, Columbus". Typically George Black decided this was too simple. Before Trinder realised what was happening, Black had signed up Edmundo Ross and his orchestra and commissioned a spectacular Cuban set. Another notable turn was "The Jackdaw of Rheims" with music by Herman Finck.

Came 1944, the troops were advancing in Normandy and victory was in the air. George Black's streak of patriotism came to the fore with his next Palladium show "Happy and Glorious". He also gave it speed, brilliance, beauty and fun, the latter in the person of Tommy Trinder again. Trinder impersonated Frank Sinatra in front of a microphone wilting in sheer ecstasy.

Soon after the declaration of war, George Black had extended his sphere to include the Hippodrome. He opened in March, 1939 with "Black and Blue" . He defied all reasonable belief by declaring it to be an "intimate revue". Hardly at the Palladium. Hardly since the producer was Robert Nesbitt. He had worked for Charlot and had developed a highly systematic and disciplined approach to production with timetable, work load and costings all worked out even before the first rehearsal. It was in complete contrast to the traditionally haphazard methods in the theatre. Nesbit's methods were exactly suited to reduce the heavy overheads in Black's spectacular revues. The cast pivoted around Vic Oliver and Francis Day who "floated through the evening in a series of frothy gowns and an expression of demure mischief". The gowns were at their frothiest and her expression at its most demure as a Victorian bride undressing, removing first her crinoline and then layer upon layer of tempestuous petticoats, eventually coming to some very frilly frillies. She also gave her impression of what would happen if Elizabeth Bergner, as the Boy David, and Anna Neagle as Queen Victoria, were to be rivals in auditioning for the role of Scarlet O'Hara. By the end of the evening she was coaxing the audience into joining in choruses, giving dolls to those who sang well. To those she thought were singing badly she handed out prizes of varying inconvenience ranging from a zinc bath to a roll of wire netting. Max Wall appeared as an art gallery attendant holding forth at length with his opinion on the old masters.

Continuing with his pun titles, "Black Velvet" opened in November 1939 It included the Cole Porter song "My Heart Belongs to Daddy". In America it had been sung by Mary Martin doing a strip tease under a mink coat. Typically Black had it sung by four leading ladies, Roma Beaumont, Roberta Hubby, Norma Dawn and Carole Lynn. Not only were they wearing mink coats, but hats and muffs as well and all designed by London's top designer, Norman Hartnol. Also there was Vic Oliver, with his violin trying to play "Roses of Piccardy" while at odds with the whole Hippodrome orchestra. Finale to the first act was "Meet the Stars at the Cafe Royal" notably with Roma Beaumont as Vesta Victoria and Gabrielle Brune as Vesta Tilley. As a finale it was particularly striking for it was all in black. As a climax the whole cast invaded the auditorium and persuaded the audience to partner them in the polka.

Third in the series was "Black Vanities", which opened in April 1941 though this time it was at the Victoria Palace. It was described as "full of colour, movement and humour, a little dancing, some pretty songs and sketches and, above all, Bud Flanagan". Without the usual gang distractions, he surprised the audience with an unsuspected ability for impersonations. He also played the part of a beachcomber and appeared in a skit on "Rain", Somerset Maugham's steamy tale of sexual desire in the monsoon.

Black staged a series of revues at the Prince of Wales. Three were built around Sid Field. He arrived completely unknown in the West End yet was a fully mature comedian. A twenty seven year contract had kept him bound to the provinces. Immediately it expired, Black starred him in "Strike a New Note". He became famous overnight.

A large, lumbering man, he did not have a funny face but his plastic features would suddenly change into a friendly smile, though accompanied by a sidelong, rather bashful, look that seemed to take the audience into his confidence. His characters were full of blustering self confidence only to be suddenly robbed of all pretensions when confronted by some disaster.

In "Strike a New Note", he introduced one of his most famous characters Slasher Green. Complete in wide-shouldered, spiv length coat and cockney accent, he portrayed a type he had carefully studied in Soho. But despite the outward swagger he still managed to endow the character with all the pathos of the helpless coward.

Sid Field's other forte was the sporting sketch. In many ways it was akin to Harry Tate, but with the slickness of modern comedy and with Gerry Desmond as stooge. In this revue he was learning to play golf. "Get behind the ball" Desmond commanded. His response was exactly what Harry Tate would have said "But it's the ball all round".

Also in "Strike a New Note" there was Zoe Gail, making her first hit with the song "I'm Going to Get Lit up". With the concentrated wit, which few songs possess, it, surprisingly, raised the ire of the powerful critic James Agate:

As soon as the note started fading, Black struck it again in November 1944. This time Sid Field's pastime sketch was photography. It was proof of his ability that he was able to bring completely new gags to such an old subject. He did not fall over the tripod nor did he get lost in the cloth. Instead his lines included "Show me your teeth. No! no! no need to take them out".

He also appeared as an artist who's picture is being criticised by a horrid little girl until he is driven to suggest "Why don't you go and play a nice game on the railway line".

The final of the three shows George Black staged for Sid Field came in 1946 and was called "Piccadilly Hayride". Among Field's characters was a highly refined cinema organist who plays a simple little tune and then, proudly smoothing his hair, asks for requests. A voice from the dress circle asks for a fugue. His whole facade crumbles as he desperately attempts to hide his inability behind an increasingly desperate pretence at confidence. His sporting sketch was learning to play snooker. Starting as a self confident pupil, "Sure it is easy" he tries to cover up his increasingly obvious inability by assaulting the marker. But nothing can hide his shame when he puts his cue not only through the cloth but through the complete table.

In each of the Sid Field revues, George Black also gave a chance to a newcomer. In "Piccadilly Hayride" Terry Thomas seized his opportunity as a suave and blasé BBC disc jockey who has forgotten to bring the records. So he has to impersonate singers, meeting his Waterloo when it came to Paul Robson.

Soon after the run both Sid Field and George Black were dead. His place in the Moss Empire was taken by Val Parnell. But Parnell was content to remain strictly the impresario and he veered more and more towards music hall with three week stands at the Palladium by stars, mainly from the United States.

CHAPTER VII
CURTAINS ON COMEDY

It is rather surprising that in the 'thirties, not withstanding the sensation caused by the energy of the chorus in "No No Nanette", British audiences were still flocking to traditional musical comedy. Certainly the productions had moved on from the days of George Edwardes. But comedy remained uppermost. Following in the steps of W.H.Berry, the new batch of comedians notably Stanley Lupino, Bobby Howes and Leslie Henson, became the major, indeed almost the only, attraction. The leading young man, young lady, the chorus, decor, music and dancing, all were relegated to become a background for the antics of the comedian. Each had a supporting comedian , such as Laddie Cliff, Wylie Watson and Richard Hearne, who were more companions in fun rather than the conventional stooges. Leslie Henson had two, Richard Hearne and Fred Emney. Furthermore each group included a heavyweight lady: Lupino and Cliff were in mortal fear of Eileen Munro. The diminutive Bobby Howes was being constantly demeaned by two formidable ladies, Vera Pearce and Bertha Belmore. Leslie Henson also acquired a heavyweight, but it was in the massive form of Fred Emney.

Consequently the shows depended almost entirely on the inventiveness of the comedian. During rehearsals for the pre-London tour, Leslie Henson would scour the local shops for items he could turn into amusing props. Like the others he would still be developing his part not only during rehearsals but even during the run. Bobby Howes liked to try out his new jokes on matinee audiences. The art lay in making well rehearsed incidents and trite dialogue seem spontaneous. It required a high degree of timing, team work and give and take.

Almost by coincidence these groups found their response to the demand for greater energy lay with the acrobats within their company. The most obvious example was Richard Hearne. He had been on stage as a child alongside his father who actually was an acrobat. So he was always diving through windows and sliding down ladders, made all the more surprising since he made up as an old man.

Stanley Lupino had also seriously trained as an acrobat. He could fall down and get up again with such agility it looked as though he had bounced. It was an ability he held in common with his cousin Lupino Lane. Much of the appeal of "Me and My Girl" lay in Lane's somersaults down stairs while in his ermine and velvet robes. Bobby Howes had also trained as an acrobat, otherwise he would never have withstood the punishment meted out to him by his two hefty support ladies.

Just as of old, after the author had established some semblance of credibility, the plot was of little or no consequence. Indeed the author's work was now considerably simplified. All the intricate dove-tailing required of the Gaiety authors was no longer necessary. The supremacy of the comedian relegated the hero and heroine almost into non-existence. Each with his "feed", could carry complete scenes on their own. There was on longer need for the "Big Six" statuesque girls to be in the background, nor for outsize gangsters nor even speciality mummers or dancers to provide relief. The running order was simply scene with the comedians alternating with scene with the chorus.

Unlike revue, the lyrics were mundane, almost nursery rhymes, in their simplicity such as "Oh, I don' want to go to bed" repeated three times in different keys. It was of no consequence for it was difficult to hear the words the chorus were singing. There might be one comedy lyric allowing the comedian to make asides and facial expressions. Typical was Stanly Lupino's "I lift up my finger and I say tweet tweet, sush sush, now now, come come" It allowed him to practice his skill in persuading even the most recalcitrant of audiences to join in. He allocated a pair of words to each section of the audience, the stalls, dress circle, upper circle and, always most responsive, the gallery.

There had to be one simple and catchy tune to send the audience home humming. The other numbers merely provide suitable background to keep the chorus tapping.

By the 'thirties, long dresses had come back into fashion. So the chorus had to abandon all the charlstoning and high kicks they had danced so enthusiastically through the flapper 'twenties. Instead they danced to a more leisurely tempo. Indeed C.B.Cochran started dressing his young ladies in masses of petticoats, frills and frou-frous reminiscent more of George Edwardes' day. Also, as with George Edwardes, the Young Ladies were chosen as much for their wit and intelligence as for their sex-appeal. On stage they were still divided into sedate and statuesque girls, the equivalent of the "big eight" and the livelier, petite, dainty dancers. Cochran pointed out during an interview with the press that modern make up and good lighting meant it was no longer necessary to place such importance on beauty. While he still looked for regularity of limbs, he also took into account their deportment and the way they walked.

Also at this time all dancing had fallen under the influence of Fred and Adele Astaire. Their stylish unison in a whole series of films had astonished London. They had thereby set major problems for the choreographers of musical comedies.

First there was the sophistication of these two specialist dancers. Most of the musical comedy stars had not been taught ballet nor even proper dancing. Yet, as a matter of prestige, they had to appear more proficient than the chorus. Fortunately most of them were already as good as the chorus since that is where they had started. They had made their way up to stardom through sheer diligence and proficiency so they were comparatively malleable to the new demands being made upon them.

One aspect was beyond the ingenuity of any choreographer. Dancers on the films could rest between takes or, by means of cuts, even in the middle of a routine. Consequently their dances could be far longer and more energetic. In the same way, dancers in the cinema had any amount of time to get back their breath before finishing the song or embarking on further dialogue. None of this was possible on the stage.

So choreographers working in musical comedy had to fudge the dances. They developed steps that were elaborate walking rather than dancing Also it was comparatively easy to teach ballet arm movements. Time to recover breath could be gained by having the chorus finish off the dance routine.

Space was another problem set by the cinema. Audiences accept a near empty stage in ballet; but not in musicals. The cinema complicated matters further. Film sets could have furniture and even entire walls moved while out of range of the camera thereby giving dance and dancers an uninterrupted flow.

Theatre audience now expected the same. So choreographers on the musical stage would arrange their routines around the scenery or, better still, incorporate it as part of the dance.

This development was led by a new generation of choreographers: Fred Carpenter, Joan Davies and Buddy Bradley who, back in the United States, had developed trucking and the oo-beat step. They even took the revolving stage in their stride.

STANLEY LUPINO AND LADDIE CLIFF

The first of this new generation of musical comedians was Stanley Lupino. In 1929 he embarked on a "love" series starting at the Gaiety. Lupino's technique was to bludgeon the audience with a never slackening sequence of acrobatics, props, jokes and spontaneous absurdities suggested by whatever was happening on the stage. This all out assault on the senses required a degree of skill. Lupino knew exactly how far he could go without taxing credulity and becoming absurd. He had a cockney perkiness which had a wide appeal and provided a common denominator between stalls and gallery. Hence his gift for coaxing even the most staid audiences into joining in with his songs. He had a characteristic, lacking in many leading actors, of seeming to listen to whatever was being said on the stage and registering genuine surprise at every new situation. Given his athleticism, a slap on the back he would do three somersaults in quick succession and with perfect equanimity. .

Laddie Cliff, his partner in management as well as on the stage, made an excellent sparing partner. He was shy and retiring, but with a definite gift for quiet and unexpected humour. His perfect calm was in complete contrast to Lupino's whirlwind tactics. The expressive way Cliff danced and the astonishing way Stanley tumbled made them a well matched pair.

Together they wrote the best part of the books and lyrics, showing a knack for writing as well as speaking funny lines. They were quite unabashed over reviving the corniest of jokes. A note in one of their programmes claimed that the manuscript had been found among Roman remains. The original was supposed to be in the possession of the British Museum. They believed the author had been burnt at the stake as a punishment for having written such rubbish. They also issued a warning that any attempt to try and follow the plot usually ended in lunacy

While their dialogue was almost childish in its simplicity, Lupino also wrote lyrics with a wit almost unique in musical comedy.

Hats off to Edgar Wallace,
Look what he's done for me
I long to be know as the new Sweeny Todd
I want to be chased by the whole Flying Squad
I'd love to see Laughton and Donat
Perform in a pale green lime,
With heroine shrieking
And ev'ry act reeking
Of crime, crime, crime.

I've purchased a gun and a bludgeon
Developed a cynical grin
I'm longing for someone to call be a crook

And think that I'm covered in sin.
I've already killed the canary
I've frightened two girls in the park
And now I am waiting
With heart palpitating
To strangle our cat in the dark

Their career at the Gaiety opened with "Love Lies" in march, 1929. It was originally intended as a stop gap but, in the unexpected way things happen in he theatre, it developed into a run of 347 performances. It was crammed with Lupino humour. At one point he was forced to spend the night in a dog kennel. When he emerged in the morning it was complete with a bone in his mouth.

In much the same vein there followed "The Love Race" in June 1930 and in December 1931 there was "Hold My Hand" and in March 1934, "Sporting Love" This had, as usual, an extremely involved story. Lupino produced yet another version of his dog and bone joke. He tried to hide from his creditors in a haycock. On being discovered by a bailiff armed with a pitchfork, he stood up clutching an egg crying "Don't hit me, I'm a mother.

Stanley Lupino and Laddie Cliff beseeching Eileen Munro in "Sporting Love" in 1934

Lupino and Cliff then transferred their activities to the Hippodrome. They opened in June, 1935 in "Love Laughs". It was about crooks and included a scene in the prison yard. It was an excuse to sing "Oh to be in Dartmoor, now that Spring is here". Also there was a scene set in the police station when the station officer dispatches a colleague to place a bet for him and warns him not to be caught by the constable on duty.

They next appeared at the Saville in September, 1936. The subject was hunting and the title "Over She Goes". Then in September, 1937, Stanley Lupino appeared again at the Shaftesbury in "Crazy Days". He adapted it from a book he had written in five days as a bet. The plot was hardly novel, with direct affiliation to the operetta "Madam Sherry". This time, the student in Paris persuaded an aunt rather than an uncle to increase his allowance by fictitiously claiming a wife and in due course, a child. However the situation became desperate when the aunt threatens to pay him a visit. Friends and neighbours are hastily drafted in to make up his fictional family. Several extra comedians were brought in: Eric Fawcett as an Earl, Syd Walker as a Police inspector of the tough old school and Richard Murdoch as a dandy sergeant of the new. Laddie Cliff was in the preliminary tour but, due to ill health, had to drop out before the London first night. His place was taken by Leo Franklyn. Cliff died a few weeks later.

In August 1938 Stanley Lupino returned to the London Hippodrome under the banner of George Black in "The Fleet's Lit up". Again he was not only the star but was also largely responsible for writing the book. It conformed to his usual style, but was planned to follow in the wake of the Silver Jubilee celebrations. This was made clear in the title, derived from an unfortunate lapse by one of the BBC commentators at the Spithead Review. It was also supposed to be relevant to the plot. Certainly it opened with a modern naval setting. However a flash back to Mary Read and the eighteenth century pirating days, and the story was soon lost. But not the patriotism. The first act curtain fell on a spectacular old time naval battle complete with full sound effects. Later in the evening, Stanley Lupino fought a duel. He shot the seconds, the surgeon and a rabbit that happened to be passing by, but entirely failed to hit his opponent. Then, as First Sea Lord he put in a little practical experience by sailing a toy boat on the round pond in Kensington Gardens. Also in nodding reference to the Jubilee, there was a lavish panoramic scene of the Spithead Review.

It was not until July 1941 that Stanley Lupino made his next appearance in "Lady Behave" at His Majesty's. Set in Hollywood, it was yet another quite impossible story, tailor made for his knockabout humour. The production was further enhanced by Sally Gray and Judy Campbell

LUPINO LANE

In the mean time another member of the Lupino clan had also been enhancing the family name. He was Stanley's cousin Lupino Lane and he was appearing in "Me and my Girl" at the Victoria Palace. It was an excellent example of low broad comedy. Lupino Lane played a cockney who inherits a peerage and a family castle. As Bill Snibson, he struggled valiantly with etiquette, polite conversation and the proper way to make a bow. George Graves was one of his aristocratic relatives. His period way of telling funny stories not only contrasted with Lupino's clowning but was in harmony with what was essentially an old fashioned musical. Bill Snibson horrifies all his aristocratic relations. However, by the first interval he has coerced them into doing the Lambeth Walk. And thereby hung its success

When "Me and My Girl" opened in December, 1937, the Victoria Palace had been long forgotten as a West End theatre. Theatregoers did not even know where it was. The show received an indifferent press and it was threatening to be a failure. Then the BBC broadcast an excerpt. Listeners heard the audience roaring with laughter. What was more, they heard "The Lambeth Walk". Even before the broadcast had finished the box-office telephone started ringing and it never stopped that evening. The next day there was a long queue outside the theatre - overnight business quadrupled, and its run of 1,646 performances assured.

Noel Gay, who's real name was Reginald Armitage, made eight attempts at composing "The Lambeth Walk" before he was satisfied with it. It proved a perfect example of his technique of repeating a simple catchy phrase sometimes three or four times over. But he had no idea it would be a hit song and certainly not that it would become a perennial success.

A simplified version of the rather complicated stage dance was introduced into the chain of Locarno Dance halls and soon became a great favourite. It was one of the first dances since the quadrille where the partners separated.

The two cousins, Stanley Lupino and Lupino Lane joined forces for "La di di da". It opened at the Victoria Palace in March 1942. Actually Stanley Lupino only wrote the book and ensured that Lupino Lane had a worthy hackneyed successor to "Me and My Girl". The story centred around a stolen necklace. There were four imitations also going the rounds.

It was followed at the Victoria Palace in April, 1944 with "Meet Me Victoria". Here Lupino Lane started as a porter. Enter a powerful female from the Continent, looking for a husband so that she can claim British citizenship. Her eye falls on the little porter who naively accepts her invitation to join her at the buffet. Sitting on the stool, he performed apparently gravity defying antics to avoid her overwhelming advances. The plot thickens with the appearance of Lupino's true love and gives rise to a pert little song entitled "You're a nice little baggage". However the lady's marriage papers are found to be out of order and this is considered sufficient display of initiative for the little porter to be promoted station master.

BOBBY HOWES

An indication of the way musical comedy was to develop had been shown back in 1931. The Clayton and Waller management team had come into prominence when they bought the British rights of "No No Nanette" even before it had reached Broadway. After importing one or two more American shows they concluded they could provide just as good a product homemade. But even this innovation started to pall and Herbert Clayton left to direct films. So Jack Waller continued on his own producing a series of musicals at the Saville. The books were by R.P. Weston and Bert Lee and Jack Waller, helped by Joseph Tunbridge, provide the music. Altogether they tailor made a vehicle ideal for Bobby Howes.

He made an early appearance in concert parties. Audience participation plays a vital part in this and strengthened his personality in his musicals. The character of the diminutive Bobby Howes was a blatant boyishness which appealed particularly to middle aged ladies in the audience. He would race about the stage, constantly up to some mischief. Then, whenever he got into a scrape he would disarm all attempts to admonish him by assuming a shining innocence. But behind this lay real acting ability as was shown in his impersonations which could range from a penguin to a racing cox.

His first essay into revue had been in "The Little Revue" and "The Second Little Revue". Only the year before he had made an outstanding success in the musical comedy "Mr. Cinders".

To start with Bobby Howes was partnered with Wylie Watson. "For the Love of Mike" opened in October 1931. It was based on a farce about burglary which Waller had seen in the provinces. Despite this inappropriate subject matter, he had been impressed but felt it needed music. Bobby Howes, along with Alfred Drayton, were the burglars and were quickly caught and sentenced. This conveniently led to one of Waller's songs "The Prison Blues". However the crook element barely lasted the first act. After that it was simply Bobby Howes let loose. At one point, he caught his foot in the back of an armchair. Never could there have been such contortions to get a foot free.

At this time Jack Waller was experimenting with the chorus. In "For the Love of Mike" he abolished it altogether. Instead members of the orchestra helped out on the few occasions when any singing was needed. In the later show "Yes Madam", he even reverted to the ancient Greek method. The chorus was completely divorced from the action and just chanted apt comments as the story unfolded.

In June, 1932, there followed "Tell her the Truth" which was the mixture as before. Although it was supposed to have been adapted, it had little in common with the book "Nothing But the Truth". Bobby Howes would win a thousand pounds if he did not lie for twenty four hours. Of course during that period he was asked any number of important and delicate questions. He was even forced to tell the Vicar's daughter that he thought she sang appallingly

In March 1933 there followed "He Wanted Adventure" based on the play "Ambrose Applejohn's Adventure"

After this show Jack Waller moved his company over to the Hippodrome. For this much larger theatre, the comedy element was enlarged in both senses of the word. The new arrivals were Vera Pearce and Bertha Belmore. Bertha Belmore managed to give stability to the productions. She would remain calm and collected whilst chaos and riot whirled around her.

Vera Pearce was a modern version of Connie Ediss. She had spent years in the music hall and burlesque. She had bulk and made much physical play with it. They opened at the Hippodrome in September 1934 in "Yes Madam". Here Bobby Howes and Vera Pearce executed a dance called Czechoslovak Love. It entailed the diminutive Bobby Howes being flung to the farthest corners of the stage by the grim bulk of Vera Pearce. Somehow he always managed to land safely and gamely return for more.

It became an essential part of the formula.

"Yes Madam" was a technical improvement on its predecessors. The jokes and situations were not contrived but developed naturally from the story. The cast were instructed not to go out of their way to get laughs and, in compensation, they were given sound characterisations. Once again the story was founded on a book. Bobby Howes and Binnie Hale could inherit a fortune on condition they stayed in domestic service for at least two months. In any ordinary household they would have been sacked within two minutes.. But for the sake of the play, they managed just to accomplish the task.

The next piece was "Please Teacher" and opened at the Hippodrome in October 1935. It was another play about an inheritance and caused Wilson Disher to remark "Where there's a will there's a play". This time Bobby Howes had an aunt who had hidden her will in, of all impractical places, a statue of Napoleon, somewhere in a girl's school. As an establishment for young ladies it proved truly amazing. There were joint head mistresses , Miss Trundle (Vera Pearce)and Miss

Pink, (Bertha Belmore) Also there was a music master, Mr. Clutterbuck (Wylie Watson). During the course of his stay there, Bobby Howes came under the instruction of Vera Pearce for a period in the gymnasium. She showed herself in great form forcing him to work out on the parallel bars. Later he had to spend a night in the school and was caught, after lights out, searching for the will in the dormitories. He hastily pretended he was sleep walking. There was an agile chorus of young ladies who did a fetching little dormitory dance, placing their candles on the floor and then jumping over them

Howes under gymnastic supervision from Vera Pearce in "Please Teacher" in 1935

Jack Waller and Joseph Tunbridge created what almost amounted to a precedent. In a programme note, they openly admitted their indebtedness to Beethoven and Tchaikovsky.

After a brief interval, the company was back in February 1937 in "Big Business". It certainly lived up to its title and the mixture was the same as before. Almost. There was a subtle difference in that Bobby Howes was bowing to the passing years. He became less winsome and more slapdash. Consequently his performance won him wider appeal. Also it abandoned all attempt to give a reason for the various situations. Everyone seemed to do just whatever they liked but, because the company had been together for so long, the skill of their interplay carried the audience with it. In his customary scene with Vera Pearce, Bobby Howes was subjected to vigorous beauty treatment. Also there was a pageant in which Bobby Howes, as a genuinely little Little John, was in constant danger of being lacerated by his two massive whirling leading ladies. As usual, he somehow managed to survive. Then there was Wylie Watson as a detective. At one point it was necessary for him to assume a disguise, so he chose to be an armchair. But disaster, for who should sit down in his arms but Vera Pearce - instant collapse. After this awkward incident, the armchair was put to considerable trouble sidestepping threatened repitions.

In October, 1937 Bobby Howes teamed up with Cicely Courtneidge at the Hippodrome in "Hide and Seek". It was a musical conceived of a wealth of experience. The book was by Guy Bolton who had written twenty five musicals. Fred Thompson was a runner up with twenty three and Douglas Furber with seventeen. The music and lyrics were by Vivian Ellis, a contributor to the scores of more than twenty musicals. The fruit of all this experience was a story about a jockey's love for the barmaid at "The Running Horse" inn at Epsom. It was spread over two generations, the 1890's and the present day. The composer provided the hit tune "She's my Lovely"

LESLIE HENSON

During the twenty years he had been on the stage, Henson never appeared in a flop. The reason was simple. No matter how poor the material his fertile imagination and comic genius made the most stock situation seem completely novel and hilariously funny. Now he was recruited by Firth Shepherd for a series starting at the Gaiety. Firth Shepherd made sure he was given every opportunity including a versatile partner Richard Hearne. Douglas Furber brought his harp to the party as lyrist and was also author-in-chief.

The first show was called "Nice Goings On" and opened at the Strand in September 1933. It was about civil servants in a Scandinavian country. Sentiment was cut to a minimum allowing the piece to depend almost entirely on anecdote and fantastic invention.

This was followed by "Lucky Break" in October 1934. The plot figured a folding bed which was constantly shutting into the wall. However Leslie Henson always managed to bluff his way out of the compromising situations. At one point he had to frighten away an old lady. He did it to great effect by pretending to be mad. His eyes stood out on stalks and simultaneously he squinted. he tore the stuffing out of a footstool and proceeded to eat it, seemingly with relish. The old lady fled. He also sang one of his songs with Heather Thatcher slung like an astrakhan collar around his shoulders and all the time Richard Hearne was making entrances by sliding down ladders and exits by diving head first through windows.

After this show Firth Shepherd and his company moved across the street to the Gaiety, taking over where Stanley Lupino and Laddie Cliff had left off. They were joined by Fred Emney junior. Unlike his father, the son was vast, monumental and sublimely cool. He knew how to make the best of poor material, often using his hands to give point to lines that were only moderately funny. He could build credible characters out of lifeless parts. He made an excellent foil to Leslie Henson.

A young couple, Louise Browne and Roy Royston, also joined the company. Louise Browne had been in the Ziegfeld Shows. She was beautiful besides being a good actress. She had an attractive personality and a pleasant voice. Added to all this she was a first class ballet dancer. Fred Thompson and Guy Bolton were recalled to help Douglas Furber. Debroy Somers led the resident band.

The first of the new series opened in October 1935 and was called "Seeing Stars". Florence Desmond was in the cast. The story concerned the crown jewels, which were stolen, as were Leslie Henson's trousers. Henson was a fake fortune teller and Fred Emney, in a huge striped jersey, was an exiled king residing in the Rivera.

In "Swing Along" in September, 1936, Leslie Henson this time lost his shirt. It was all highly topical with the black shirts and brown shirts strutting the Continent. As a fanatical gambler with massive debts, Henson had to impersonate Xabiski, leader of the yellow shirts. Then he found himself in his hotel bedroom surrounded by the No Shirts. To escape he had to impersonate Xabiski's bride, a thoroughly unconvincing lady wearing the hotel's lace curtains. On another occasion, Fred Emney tried to take his photograph. His camera had a long bellows which straggled from the tripod down onto the ground like an immense caterpillar. Finally they formed the Gresham Narkington Quartet, a skit on the Gershwin Parkington Quartet. Louise Browne played the accordion at great danger to herself. Fred Emney played the piano, Leslie Henson struggled with a double base whilst Richard Hearne got entangled with a french horn which coiled round and round his waist like a cobra. Eventually he had to summon Leslie Henson to his aid who, needless to say, only made matters worse.

The next production was called "Going Greek" and opened in September 1937. The curtain rose to reveal a Greek mountainside. A meeting of the shareholders of Bandits Ltd, was in progress. It was a stormy meeting too, and things did not look so good for the directors Leslie Henson and Fred Emney. Kidnapping was going through a slump. The company's only asset was a very drunk opera singer. "What are you going to do to me?" Richard Hearne querulously asked. "The Lord Chamberlain has cut out the reply to that one" Henson replied. To make matters worse, the opera singer was enjoying life on the Greek mountainside and did not want to be ransomed. So all three decided to double-cross the shareholders. This made it necessary to assume a variety of disguises. These included a company of strolling players in classical Greek attire and playing harps, schoolboys in shorts and Eton collars, sucking lollipops and playing conkers.

Leslie Henson conducts the annual general meeting of Bandits Ltd. in "Going Greek" in 1937

Finally Henson transformed himself into a wedding cake. He also had to mouth the words to a record of "Rigoletto" played off stage. He was completely flummoxed when the voice of a soprano suddenly joined in. "Going Greek" had to be taken off prematurely as Henson fell ill.

After a few weeks holiday the company reassembled in August 1938 for "Running Riot". At this time the company consisted of Leslie Henson, Richard Hearne, Fred Emney, Louise Brown and Roy Royston. On the staff side were Douglas Further and Guy Bolton. Fred Thompson had left after contributing to "Going Greek". Debroy Somers and his band were still in residence.

In "Running Riot" kidnapping was still the name of the game. This time it was a boy film star who was held for ransome. And that was about as far as the story ever got. At one point, all three, Henson, Emney and Hearne, where smuggling through customs a suitcase full of clocks on which duty should have been paid. Having said they had nothing to declare they were put to extreme embarrassment as it turned mid-day. There were chimes, tings, cuckoos and even the dong of a grandfather clock. Later in the evening Henson took part in a sextet, but he seemed to find great difficulty in keeping up with the rest. Richard Hearne also danced the Lancers with an imaginary partner, who was evidently not very good.

It so happened that "Running Riot" was destined to be the last show staged at the Gaiety. As had been the case with the earlier theatre, Town Planning ordained that it should be pulled down. Then came the war and the plan was at first postponed and finally abandoned. In the mean time the Gaiety Theatre had suffered in the blitz and was falling into disrepair. After the war Lupino Lane bought it and began to restore it but it was too great an expense. After a brave struggle he had to abandon the project. Finally it was sold and pulled down.

JACK HULBERT AND CICELY COURTNEIDGE

After playing apart in variety and in revue the Hulberts came together again in 1938 for a series of musicals at the Palace. Their combined performance had always shown a harmony that comes only from long practice and mutual understanding. As a rule, Jack Hulbert did the impertinent thing whilst Cicely Courtneidge was ever ready with the pertinent comment. She always had unquestioned authority over the opposite sex.

Directly she appeared on the scene, no one was left in any doubt that the real business of the evening had begun. Everyone on the stage immediately got busy. Little surprise, then, that she was known, even off stage, as The Colonel. However, having once established her authority, Cicely would let herself get caught up in the story and play the fool most expertly. She would set out on some project with almost every sign of grim determination. Yet she never quite succeeded in hiding a certain inner doubt. She could make her effect, even in the largest theatre, with the minimum effort - a wink, a shrug of the shoulders so that, with her perfect sense off timing, the meaning was made clear. Becoming sentimental, indeed almost moving, she would let the merest hint of irony creep into her voice or, more obviously, by uttering one of her high squeaks or hoarse gutturals.

Jack Hulbert was an actor in the George Grossmith - Jack Buchanan tradition. However, by playing second fiddle to his wife his humour was less obvious. With good natured high spirits and a debonair charm, he was a nimble dancer, once described as "the traditional clown's face, seemingly hung by wires, over rhythmically pattering feet".

Jack Hulbert was one of the most energetic producers of musical comedy, a quality he duly transmitted to the chorus, well drilled, lively, intelligent and very much up to the mark. He also wrote the books for their shows giving them a sound technical construction. He was usually assisted by Arthur Macrae the author of several successful comedies including "Indoor Fireworks" and "Travellers Joy". His broad comedy, garnished with sophisticated dialogue, was in just the right style for the Hulberts. He would develop a simple foible into a complete character study.

For the first three shows, Jack Hulbert and Arthur Macrae were joined by yet a third author, Archie Menzies. Their first concerted effort with music by Vivian Ellis was "Under your Hat" which opened at the Palace in November, 1938.

It was one of several musicals, starting with "Bitter Sweet", which set out to bring in the songs naturally. In practice, in "Under Your Hat" it was no more than the provision of excuses for Jack and Cicely to set off on some chase requiring them to assume a variety of disguises. In this case they were trying to recover the prototype aeroplane carburettor stolen by a spy. Events followed each other so fast that the audience never had time to think, which was just as well for it was all very absurd. Whenever the story was in danger of flagging, the plot would take a new twist and everyone would rush off on some further wild goose chase. In the pursuit of this spy Cicely started as a jealous film star, wearing such a tight dress she could not sit down. Later she was the essence of experienced naughtiness having supper in a private room. Next she was a vivacious French maid, then in a beach skirt, a greasy mechanic and finally as Mrs. Sheepshanks, wife of a Colonel in the Indian Army. . As a distinguished visitor to a finishing school she led the girls in singing "The Empire Depends on You".

"Under Your Hat" closed on the outbreak of war but reopened in October 1940 and continued to run for a total of 512 performances.

After a tour, the Hulberts returned to the Palace in April, 1942 in "Full Swing". This was another spy story. - A dossier on cabaret in South America had gone astray. Its importance rested, no doubt, on the assumption that all artistes in that region were Mata Hari type spies. Together they pursued a sinister Dr. Carlos (Kenneth Kent) and his ravishing accomplice Carole Markoff (Nora Swinburn). The similarity in plot gave them similar opportunities for appearing in disguises. But for the most part Cicely Courtneidge was an irate leading lady rehearsing an incompetent chorus. This proffered the excuse for introducing all the songs and dances. The total effect was nearer a comedy with music than a musical comedy.

In September 1943, there followed "Something in the Air". The treasure hunt theme now reached its third edition. Jack Hulbert, in the Royal Air Force, and Cicely Courtneidge, in the Women's Auxiliary Air Force, are on leave when they grow suspicious of an escaped German airman. In their anxiety to capture him they overstay their leave and were, in turn, shadowed by a sergeant (Ronald Shiner)

The music was by Manning Sherwin, who had already had a successful career in Hollywood and had come to England just before the war. It was not long before Sherwin made his name here with such songs as "A Nightingale Sang in Berkley Square". He wrote part or all the scores for three Hulbert shows, but he failed to contribute a memorable number to any of them.

In November, 1945, Cicely appeared in "Under the Counter" at the Phoenix. Jack Hulbert did not have a part although he was the producer. Nor did he have a hand in the book, that being the sole work of Arthur Macrae. Again he took a topical situation and drew it out into an hilarious evening. Cicely, aided and abetted this time by Thorley Walters, appeared as a patron of the black market in a big way. There was more plot than usual and less music. Such songs as there were, were introduced under the old guise of chorus rehearsals in the leading lady's flat. The set, though, was given a new angle - three angles in fact. Each was the same room but shown from a different side.

Jack Hulbert and Cicely Courtneidge prepare a bombshell in "Under Your Hat" in 1939

Cicely Courtneidge's next West End appearance was again without Jack Hulbert. The show was called "Her Excellency" and it opened at the Hippodrome in June 1949. It was Archie Menzies's turn to provide the book. But a lady ambassador negotiating a meat contract with a South American country does not offer much scope for appearing in a rapid series of disguises. However that did not prevent Cicely from working in an impression of flying over the pyramids, the first careless rapture turning to distress as air sickness takes over. Likewise she did an impersonation of a week-end cyclist struggling up hill.

Nostalgia, for reason quite outside the story, dominated her next musical. More than twenty years before, Ivor Novello had promised to write her a musical. But it was not until 1950 that the promise materialised as "Gay's the Word". Once again Cicely was a dominant leading lady, this time head of a drama school with songs introduced under the guise of drilling a recalcitrant chorus. It was the first time Novello had written a musical with strong comedy since his score for W.H.Berry's "The Golden Moth". He used his lyrist to distance himself from his reputation for period lush romance. A chorus of "Ruritanian" guards sang "Ivor Novello's the only fellow who still believes in us". In another song the lilacs gathered in "Perchance to Dream" were compared to the Green ones that subsequently grew into "Oklahoma". His nostalgic songs now took on a different tone notably in "If Only He'd Looked My Way".

It was a big success but proved to be a sad finale. It was the last musical Cicely appeared in and the last score Novello wrote.

Indeed musical comedy as a whole was in decline. Prince and Emile Littler who ruled the lighter part of the West End theatre, sought safety through adaptations of previous comedies. Songs grafted on to an old script do not have the spontaneity of team creation that had always been the hall mark of musical comedy. Above all, these preconceived scripts forced the comedians to conform to a discipline foreign to the entire concept. Fred Emney was the only post war star who had previous experience of musical comedy and to a degree he recaptured that sprit in "Blue for a Boy", a musical version of "Its a Boy". The other comedians had all developed their style in films or television. There were exceptions. George Formby simply superimposed his real Lancastrian self in "Zip Goes a Million", a version of "Brewster's Millions". The formula was even used by the Americans. None the less, Norman Wisdom was unable to separate the undergraduate romping in " Charley's Aunt" from his winsome downtrodden little man. Perhaps the most successful was Frankie Howard. But then "A Funny Thing Happened on the Way to the Forum" was based on comedies written in a dead language two and a half thousand years before.

The real problem was the coming of television. At first the humour and sheer joy of The Two Ronnies and Morecambe and Wise meant people could have all the pleasure of musical comedy without having to go up to the West End. They did not even have to pay for increasingly expensive seats. They could enjoy it in their sitting room. But things changed and the stand up comedian took over. With the comedian anchored in front of a microphone the jokes become incidental linked by dialogue but with little logical continuity. Consequently this type of comedian depends on individual jokes. He does not have a story which can carry an audience from comic situation to comic situation, each helping fuel laughter for the next till it reaches a crescendo for the final curtain.

CHAPTER VIII
THE FINAL REVUE

Revue also suffered a marked decline after the end of the Second World War. A major exception was The Crazy Gang, now taken over by the band leader and erstwhile participant in the Palladium shows, Jack Hylton. He took them to new heights at the Victoria Palace. A similar bequest occurred with intimate revue. Charlot's mantle fell on Laurier Lister who staged six mainly successful revues;. Too few, though, for him to reach equal eminence.

JACK HYLTON & THE CRAZY GANG

The first Jack Hylton presentation of the Crazy Gang was called, appropriately enough "Together Again". It opened at the Victoria Palace in April, 1947. Even the most priggish critics acknowledged the gang were an institution and realised they would antagonise too many readers if they were anything but magnanimous. Several were content to point out the Gang's average age was 57. "Most of the jokes they play on one another were old when they were young". Anthony Cookman wrote in "The Tatler": "The aisle is full of noise, so too is a box. As far as the stage, it is in perpetual clamour. We are at a family re-union of the Crazy Gang. The gibbering years in the Palladium age is restored in Pimlico". Another critic warned readers: "Playgoers rash enough to buy the best seats may find themselves in receipt of awkward gifts or being searched for an escaped performing flea". .

A typical scene had Zena Dell smart in white tie, top hat and tails desperately trying to impersonate Hetty King singing "Burlington Bertie of Bow". What hope when behind her all five of the gang were lined up as a row of preposterous Teddy Boy Berties.

The gang continued to occupy the Victoria Palace for nearly 10 years. In 1950 there was "Young in Heart". This time Eddy Gray juggled with plates (when they were not greased). Occasionally he would send one hurtling into the wings with a viciousness that suggested there was someone there he did not like.

In October 1952, came "Ring Out The Bells". They were celebrating not only the Queen's Silver Jubilee but their own 21st anniversary. " Under this pretext they raced about the theatre in coronets and ermine, even before the curtain had gone up" reported Anthony Cookman. The only direct reference to the Royal anniversary depicted the lion and the unicorn. In this version, however, a diminutive and timid unicorn was being confronted by four highly rampant lions The gang also appeared as baby sitters; four petrifying old ladies leering as they produced foot long safety pins and monster thermometers. The much "sat-on" baby was in a large bassinet and proved to be Charlie Naughton. A choir of the sweetest schoolgirls serenaded "This is Flora's

Birthday", only to be rudely interrupted by the Gang bursting through the backdrop this time they were dressed as gross nymphs and shepherdesses.

The series came to a final and triumphant finish with " Jokers Wild" which opened in December 1954. It was noticeably more spectacular and indeed the sets tended to overwhelm the slapstick. The truth was the gang were beginning to acknowledge their years. But the slapstick was still very much in evidence. This time the girl running screaming across the stage was wearing a seriously fraying sweater. Close behind came Jimmy Gold, vigorously winding up a large ball of wool. Flanagan sang one of his monstrously deflationary songs "Wonderful, Wonderful Wolverhampton". There was a performance of the television game "What's My Line" and what a performance. Flanagan was Gilbert Harding, Charlie Naughton as Lady Barnet-by-Pass and Jimmy Nervo as Barbara Kelly who had become a rather peculiar pear shape. But all the skill that lay behind the gang's apparent buffoonery was shown with five monks solemnly ringing their monastery bells. Then slowly, almost imperceptibly, the tempo increased. They got faster and faster till the gang were performing a wild maypole dance swinging on the ropes. Then, suddenly the Abbot appeared and immediately they returned to the grave monks as before.

While the Crazy Gang could most certainly hold their own, conventional revue was suffering through rivalry from the airwaves First there was the wireless. For some years it had been reaching millions of homes. Now, however, there emerged some enormously popular variety programmes. There was "Monday Night at Eight" while with ITMA Tommy Handley reached almost every home in wartime Britain. Who, then, wanted to brave the blackout and sometimes bombs only to find the same blend of speed and comedy they could hear in their own sitting room?

The answer was a lot of people. They were to be found wherever the stars were talented and the material of quality. These audiences were not only highly selective but, as during the Great War, they had become more cynical. Consequently the sketches became much sharper. They found their idol in Hermione Gingold and loyally followed her from December 1938 in "The Gate Revue" at Notting Hill, through the blitz, the buz bombs and into victory and into 1946 and "Sweetest and Lowest" at the Ambassadors . Norman Marshall largely built them around largely Hermione Gingold. When it was being transferred to the West End, Marshall was put under considerable pressure to replace her with a star name. He resisted with the result she soon became a super star in her own right. The audience revelled in the way, as described by T.C.Worsley: "her tongue rolling around a familiar name and then quickly dropping it off with all the mud sticking on, is to watch art raising a foible to the statue of humour".

Yet the revues still had to rely on the goodwill of fellow thespians. The comments made in her series of Poisoned Ivy sketches, were classically acid: "Laurence Olivier is a tour de force but poor Donald Wolfit is forced to tour". Another time, she completed her order to the waiter: "and a saucer of milk for Dame Lilian". When her co-conspirator Hermione Baddeley asked "Who's that talking to J.B.Priestly?" Gingold replied "Not talking, listening, dear". J.B.Priestly complained bitterly. But, as the producer, Norman Marshall remarked "Half of the West End stars are complaining of the way they are mentioned and the other half are angry because they are not mentioned at all".

There were other, more conventional sketches. There was Gingold as a Picasso model, unhappy because she was multi-limbed and had a fish on her head. She then appeared dressed in Eton collar and jacket as Young Woodley's horridly well informed little son" .

Ronald Jeans was responsible for many of the lyrics and even with his ingenuity, had found a rich new vein in the vicissitudes of life in wartime Britain, such as the difficulty in finding a hotel room:

They're hanging in tiers

From the hall chandeliers".

She also appeared as a formidable head mistress of a school for spies. Other sketches included a hairdressing salon with the women confiding in the hairdresser as though he was a priest and they were in a confessional. Another sketch was on the women's vogue for fitness. A young Peter Ustinov did a series of impressions, wearing all the different clothes at once. As he worked his way through them he became increasingly slim. Robert Helpman also did impersonations and surprisingly did not dance at all. Despite all the problems, the demise of intimate revue extended into the post war years. The only revues that attracted large audiences had stars who had made their name on the wireless. Jimmy Edwards from "Take It From Here" and, above all, Kenneth Williams who had established his name and inimitable style in the Kenneth Horne series. He starred in several revues such as "Pieces of Eight".

There was an outstanding exception with "Cranks" in 1956 at the St.Martins. It was written and choreographed by John Cranko. A number of sketches had a surrealism quite different to the traditional sketch with a target. Some appealed simply for their appearance and sheer originality of effect. The cast of four knelt in a group in the centre of the stage moving their hands upwards to look almost like flames of a fire.

After the war many of the stars made come-backs. Unlike the Crazy Gang, they were extremely wary of how their former fans might greet them. They expected to find their appeal to audiences through nostalgia. Consequently the content incorporated a high proportion of previous successes. They sometimes seemed more like "Memorial" productions.

Jessie Matthews returned to the West End in "Made to Measure". But she seemed fearful over adverse comparison with those Pavilion years. In "Dance Little Lady" she made herself up as an older woman weaving wistfully among the masked ghosts of past young lovers. She even tried to bring the classic "Dancing on the Ceiling" up to date by singing it as though giving an audition before a bored producer. It was all completely unnecessary. When towards the end of the evening she sang "Tread softly because you are treading on my Dreams" she showed that all the old magic and childlike innocence was there, still intact.

Coward presented two reminiscent revues; "Sigh no More" which opened at the Piccadilly in September 1945 and "Sail Away" in 1962. He retained his traditional scenic collaboration with Gladys Calthrop. But he was an author still in vogue and could include a lot of new sketches. "Sigh No More" included a ballet burlesquing his virtually contemporary production of "Blithe Spirit" It was spoilt by bad dancing. Cyril Richard rolled his eyes in despair as he sang about Nina, an uncooperative girl from Argentina who resolutely refused to do the rumba. He also appeared as a retired Indian officer wondering what had happened to all the mess friends of his riotous youth.

The year after, another immaculate purveyor of revue, Jack Buchanan returned in "Fine Feathers" at the Prince of Wales. His co-star was Ethel Revnell who, fortunately, proved every bit as willing to suffer indignity as had Elsie Randolph. There was no change in Jack Buchanan's nonchalant style. He sang "Girls and Gowns", a Vivian Ellis number, relaxed and slightly bemused at all the work and determination the girls were taking over their frocks.

Cicely Courtneidge made her final appearance in revue in "Over the Moon" at the Piccadilly in 1953. Jack Hulbert remained as the producer and one critic remarked how "he adhered to the rhythm of the 'twenties, at a loose but exhilarating pace". Cicely certainly had no need to fear comparison with the past. She had not lost any of her energy; her costume changes remained as quick as ever. Singing "The King's Horses" showed her sense of timing was unimpaired. Nor had she lost her show of outrage touched with just a hint of foreboding. Her pretence at being jolly when expected to squash with five other people into a holiday caravan designed for three was obviously very thin. With marvellous change of character she also appeared as a retired colonel's wife coming to terms over spending a week booked mistakenly in a holiday camp.

Binnie Hale appeared in "The Punch Revue". No reminiscence here. She remained as bright and engaging as ever. The prestigious journal was the backer and could therefore call on its list of distinguished contributors, past and present, for material. The lyrics were by such luminaries as W.H. Auden, John Betchman, Louis McNeice and T.S.Eliot. Yet it merely proved that witticism on paper can utterly fail when sung behind footlights. Again and again on the first night, while the stalls applauded, the gallery booed.

It was not helped by a clumsy production. Before the evening was over, three of the cast had given impersonations of Johnny Rae and none of them were good. That was left to Binnie Hale herself who showed she had lost none of her astonishing versatility. First she was Crawfie's nanny, far out vying her charge's future skills in lauding the attributes of the young Princess Elizabeth. Crawfie's " shoes used to fasten in the FRONT. I know, I saw them" and "When she shut her eyes she couldn't see a thing". She went on to give devastating impersonations of a stream of celebrities descending the famous Cafe de Paris staircase; Margaret Rutherford, Marlene Dietrich, Yvonne Arnaud, Margaret Leighton and Bea Lillie. Each not so much a caricature in acid as a highly astute distillation of personality.

Bea Lillie herself crossed the Atlantic after an absence of eight years. She was to spend " an evening with her friends " at the Globe Theatre. Nightly she would be greeted by a storm of applause from her long time devotees. She acknowledged it typically with a deep bow which was just that little bit deeper and little bit longer so that it tipped over into burlesque. She revived several of her previous successes including the grand lady ordering two dozen dinner napkins. She sipped brandy with her famous invisible friend Maud, pointing out yet again that she was rotten to the core. The subtlety of her clowning with a minimum of gesture ensured her new material was as effective as the old. At one such moment, she fiddled with the scarf around her neck. Finally she gave it a suicidal pull. She clearly expected it to undo. It merely tightened. With the slightest choke in her voice, she adjured the audience "Don't panic. It will come undone - at least it always has".

All this time there had been an independent strain of revue in the West End. The intention was to provide the sharp and acid sketches of the old Theatre de Varietes. Normally this would still have been blocked by the Lord Chamberlain. The way round lay in club membership. Pay a subscription and you were beyond the Chamberlain' s jurisdiction. Consequently there opened several literally underground theatre clubs notably The Irving and The Watergate. Several of these revues were duly transferred to Shaftesbury Avenue The fact they were subjected to little alteration shows the Lord Chamberlain realised the days of censorship were numbed. When "Just Lately" was transferred to the Hippodrome as "High Spirits", a vicious sketch about apartheid was retained. Dr. Malan The South African Prime Minister was so incensed he threatened to boycott the Coronation. The Lord Chamberlain called his bluff, Dr. Malan had second thoughts and came to London after all.

LAURIER LISTER

Charlot's mantle had fallen upon Laurier Lister", though he never acquired quite such eminence. He had behind him twenty years as an actor and ten years as a playwright. He formed his company and in 1947 made his debut at the Royal Court with "Two pence Coloured". Max Adrian, seen against an Emmett backdrop of a crazy signal box, ranted against rail nationalisation. Elizabeth Welch and the inimitable Joyce Grenfell were another two who were to appear in several Lister revues.

In November the next year, Lister's " Oranges and Lemons" got no nearer the West End than the Lyric at Hammersmith. But it proved a reasonable success. Max Adrian was again at loggerheads with rail nationalisation. This time he was the driver of an express furiously offended when officials in Whitehall had mistakenly posted him to a sleepy branch line. He also appeared as a judge. His evident relish in the gory details of a horrific murder were exceeded only by his interest in the possibility of taking over the accused's flat.

Out of order, "Penny Plain" finally arrived in 1951. It proved to be no less highly coloured as witness the backcloths which made a major contribution to the fun. Osbert Lancaster depicted a gallery of singers at the Albert Hall leaving three holes in the centre for the faces of Joyce Grenfell, Rose Hill and Moira Fraser. Ronald Searle contributed a back drop for three little maids who rapidly degenerated into three horrible little girls from his St.Trinians. Emmett also contributed a backcloth while Richard Addinesll provided the score. Max Adrian appeared as an actor suffering a severe dose of 'flu but quite determined not to let his understudy have his chance. Joyce Grenfell was a serious minded young lady up from the country holding a high falutin' tete a tete with an imaginary and increasingly exasperated author. But most joyously, she became a coy Maud, clinging playfully to the french window curtains and refusing all pressing invitations to go into that garden "The dew is wet" she "hasn't got on the right shoes" and as a final admonishment "Maud wasn't born yesterday".

Airs on a Shoestring opened at the Royal Court in May 1953. It was generally held to be "agreeable and pleasurable". In fact Lister had speeded up the piece so that there was a total of 36 sketches This gave it the same advantages as the Crazy Gang. The ever busy present prevented the audience from dwelling on what had just happened. Max Adrian was dragged from the grave to shake a collecting tin in aid of the Ghouls flag day. He was also a lifetime peer on the eve of the Coronation, trying on his unfamiliar robes delivered late by the cleaners and fearful since he could not be sure which parts, if any, were missing. Patricia Lancaster was a lady bountiful disconcerted to find her work had been snatched from her by the National Health Service. The story of Benjamin Britten's life was sung by a male quintet to smart words and music by Flanders and Swan. The regular company still included Moira Fraser, Betty Marsden and Joyce Grenfell, this time as a secretary blindly in love with an exceedingly unpleasant boss.

In "Pay the Piper", December, 1954, Laurier Lister hoped to graduate to spectacular revue. He took the considerably larger Saville Theatre and, working to scale, brought in the broad music hall humour of Doris and Elsie Waters. They proved capable in the more subtle sketches such as a Miss Muffet so bossy that it was the spider that was frightened away. They embarked on the story of "The Ring" with unexpected and hitherto unrecorded and unfortunate developments. They were two Gaiety Girls, disconsolate at having failed to find peers to marry. Then Ian Wallace sang about an elephant in a zoo claiming memory loss so as to avoid carrying hordes of raucous children on its back. But the subtle sketches failed to register in the large auditorium.

However Lister could with credit set this failure against the considerable success d'estime when he presented Joyce Grenfell, as a diseuse. Virtually on her own she could hold an audience enraptured for an entire evening.

"Fresh Airs" opened at the Comedy in January 1956 Rose Hill appeared as a prima donna who takes great delight in shattering glass and even, with special effort, mirrors. She also appeared as Bacchante on a pedestal. To keep her reputation, she steps down for a little "refreshment" only to find considerable difficulty in remounting and assuming her pose. Max Adrian appeared as a matriarch in a Knightsbridge coffee bar, working with the uttermost sang froid a formidable expresso machine with fearfully hissing taps.

In "From Here to There", Laurier Lister experimented again . He set out, as several had before, to mix British and American humour. The mode was made clear in the opening sketch contrasting wealthy American tourists who have no time to see London's attractions with impoverished British tourists with no dollars to buy New York goodies. America was represented by James MacColl but his humour failed to win the audience. He was quickly replaced by the ever reliable Max Adrian. He had only to appear as a dramatic critic with horns and a swishing red tail for all humour to be restored. Lister did not make Cochran's mistake for he inserted it after the first night. Betty Marsden was a Polynesian woman not in the habit of reading newspapers. So she was rather surprised to find everyone had left the atoll. Even more to her astonishment, she found that she glowed in the dark. She also appeared as an unflappable air hostess haughtily dismissive when a passenger points out that a wing had fallen off. Even after the last engine has failed she consoled the passengers by saying how delightfully quiet it had become. June Whitfield was a child actress in a major success "The Turn of the Screw". As the run continues so the cast become increasingly disturbed at the way she is assuming dark and sensuous undertones.

Then there occurred one of those chance events that completely change an era.

It was the classic situation a of a director unexpectedly confronted with an empty theatre and no money. It was the 1959 Edinburgh Festival and through sheer intuition the director introduced a pair of undergraduates from Oxford to a pair from Cambridge. He told them to go ahead and produce something. When the curtain rose on "Beyond the Fringe" the quartet were wearing their own suites and there was no scenery. But that quartet comprised Alan Bennett, Dudley Moore, Jonathan Miller and Peter Cook.

Peter Cook was the most forceful as author but they all purposely set out to astonish and indeed shock the audience. Cook appeared as a miner convinced he could have been a judge had he not been so bad at Latin. Alan Bennett gave an impersonation, some said rather a cruel one, of the Archbishop of Canterbury in a sermon of high wind and hot air. But he was perhaps most effective with his sketch against capital punishment: "The Suspense is Killing Me"

Both Jonathan Miller and Dudley Moore preferred a more fanciful approach. Miller played Professor A.J.Ayer, conducting a philosophical discussion on a ridiculously trite basis: "Moore, how many apples have you got in that basket?"

Their entire concept was just as dependent on wit as on satire. They realised that with television providing subjects for satire that morning, any ad lib jokes would be dead by curtain up. So they did not deal so much with matters of the moment as with issues of the age. They criticised social behaviour as much as individual personalities.

The Lord Chamberlain, having nodded over apartheid in "High Spirits" now virtually fell asleep. Wisely he was allowing officialdom to catch up with public sentiment. The four were themselves surprised at how far they could go not only in twisting the Lord Chamberlain's tail but in the tolerance of the audience. It was quite rare for someone to stump out, an incident which Allan Bennett always gleefully chalked up as a plus point.

Their success was immediate and in due course they transferred to the Fortune Theatre in the West End for 1,184 performances and on to the Mayfair for a further 1,000.

It is ironic that almost immediately after revue was freed from the censorship that it had been railing against for centuries, it fell into terminal decline. As with musical comedy, the reason was television. It was so much easier to stay at home and see the same sort of show without having to pay. The television mandarins were particularly attracted to intimate revue because of the low costs.

They duly found their own group of irreverent undergraduates and gave them their head in "That Was the Week That Was".

However any hope that wit, sharp comment. and good humour would now permeate every home throughout Great Britain proved short lived. The desperate competition for high viewing figures encouraged television to seek the lowest common denominator. Mass audiences encouraged acid wit to degenerate into cruelty. "Spitting Image" used puppets as three dimension cartoon characters to accompany a heartless and vulgar script.

Unfortunately the one great attraction of both musical comedy and revue does not seem to be appreciated by the majority of viewers. An individual sitting among hundreds in a darkened auditorium abandons self consciousness and becomes subject to the cumulative effect. A joke may not seem all that funny but the laughter from all around is infectious and encourages the individual at least to smile or chuckle. There is a sense of bonding. In this way the laughter of an audience feeds upon itself. As one ridiculous situation follows another so the laughter becomes cumulative ending in helpless hysteria.

It is an experience completely foreign to a family sitting at home where a degree of self consciousness is always present.

This book has shown the close affinity that existed between musical comedy and revue. They hold many structural and facial factors in common. They both found support and success together when born towards the end of the nineteenth century. So it is sad that both should have gone into decline and together withered at the end of the twentieth century.

BIBLIOGRAPHY

Above all I must acknowledge my indebtedness to Eric Partridge, late editor of "Who's Who in the Theatre" and to the Eindhoven collection of theatre programmes and press cuttings in the Victoria and Albert Museum. Other publications include:

W.H.Berry Autobiography
William Boosey "Fifty Years of Music"
C.B.Cochran "Cock -a-Doodle-Do" and
"Secrets of a Showman"
Andre Charlot "Revue Producing"
Ciicely Courtneidge "Cicely"
Albert de Courville "I Tell You"
Noël Coward "Present Indicative"
Paul Derval "Folies Bergere"
Vivian Ellis "I'm on a See- aw"
George Grossmith "G.G.by himself"
Leslie Henson "Yours Faithfully"
Stanley Lupino "From the Stocks to the Stars"
W.MacQueen-Pope "Gaiety, Theatre of Encharntment"
Manders & Mitcheson "Revue"
Ernest Short, "Ring up the Curtain"

ILLUSTRATIONS & ACKNOWLEDGEMENTS

Most of the photographs were taken by the Stage Photo Co. and reproduced in "Play Pictorial". The stock of glass negatives was destroyed during the London Blitz A few other photographs and prints are from the author's collection.

INDEX

Lightning Source UK Ltd.
Milton Keynes UK
UKOW01f2259061217
314033UK00002B/15/P